student study
ART NOTEBOOK

Physical GEOLOGY

Plummer / McGeary

seventh edition

Wm. C. Brown Publishers

ubuque, IA Bogota Boston Buenos Aires Caracas Chicago
uilford, CT London Madrid Mexico City Sydney Toronto

 **A Times Mirror Company**

The credits section for this book begins on page 161 and
is considered an extension of the copyright page.

Copyright © 1996 Times Mirror Higher Education Group, Inc.
All rights reserved

A Times Mirror Company

ISBN 0–697–28732-7

Printed in the United States of America by Wm. C. Brown Communications, Inc.,
2460 Kerper Boulevard, Dubuque, IA 52001

10   9   8   7   6   5   4   3   2

The *Student Study Art Notebook* is designed to help you in your study of geology. The notebook contains art taken directly from the text and overhead transparencies; thus you can take notes during lectures, or jot down comments as you are reading through the chapters.

The notebook is perforated and 3-hole punched so, if you wish, you can remove sheets and put them in a binder with other study or lecture notes. Any blank pages at the end of this notebook can be used for additional notes or drawings.

We hope this notebook, used along with your text, helps to make the study of geology easier for you.

Directory of Notebook Figures

TO ACCOMPANY

PLUMMER/MCGEARY PHYSICAL GEOLOGY, 7E

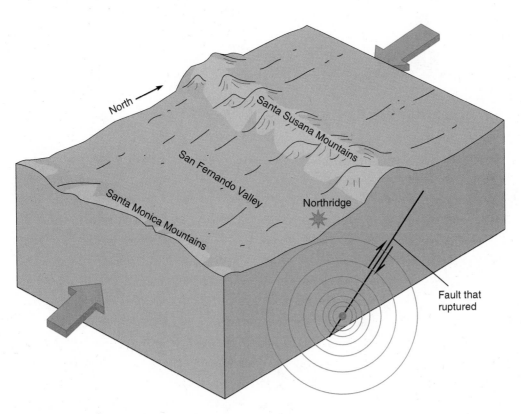

1994 Northridge Earthquake
Figure 1.2

CANADIAN ROCKIES

Chief Mtn.

COLUMBIA PLATEAU

Mt. St. Helens

CASCADE MOUNTAINS

Crater Lake

Yellowstone National Park

Teton Range

Black Hills

Mt. Shasta

Great Salt Lake

BASIN & RANGE

ROCKY MOUNTAINS

SIERRA NEVADA

COAST RANGES

Yosemite

Devil's Postpile

Bryce Canyon

Zion National Park

Death Valley

Monument Valley

Ship Rock

Mojave Desert

COLORADO PLATEAU

Los Angeles

Grand Canyon

Raiz Physiographic Map—Western Portion
Figure 1.5

2

CANADIAN SHIELD

Laurentian upland of low hills and many lakes

ADIRONDACK
MOUNTAINS

Valley & Ridge
Province

APPALACHIAN
MOUNTAINS

MISSISSIPPI RIVER

Mississippi Delta

Miami

LANDFORMS OF THE UNITED STATES

by ERWIN RAISZ   Sixth revised edition, 1957

Scale   50   100   150   200 Miles
         0   100   200 Kilometers

**Raiz Physiographic
Map—Eastern Portion**
Figure 1.5

3

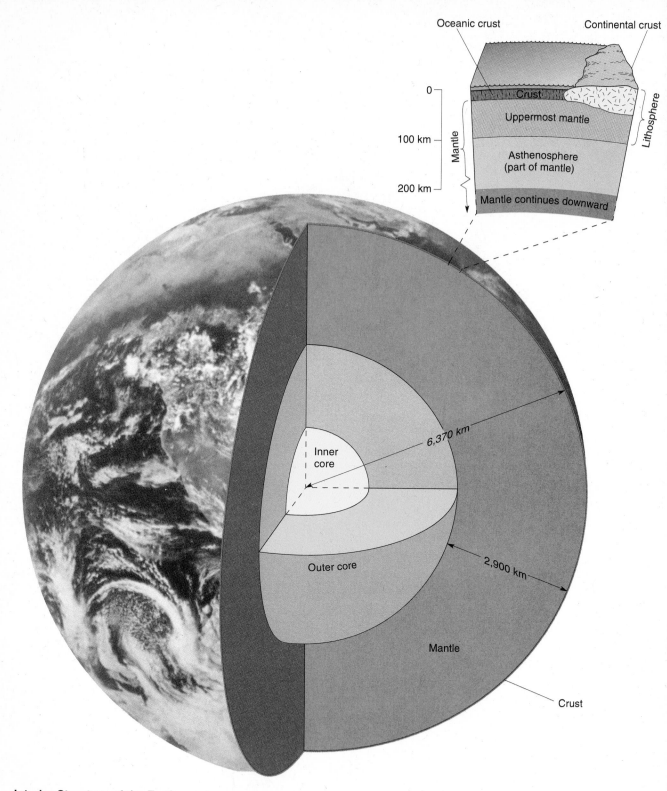

Interior Structure of the Earth
Figure 1.8

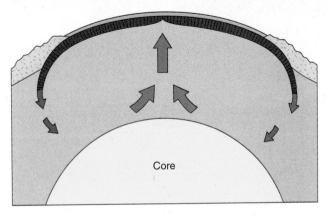

Mantle Convection
Figure 1.9

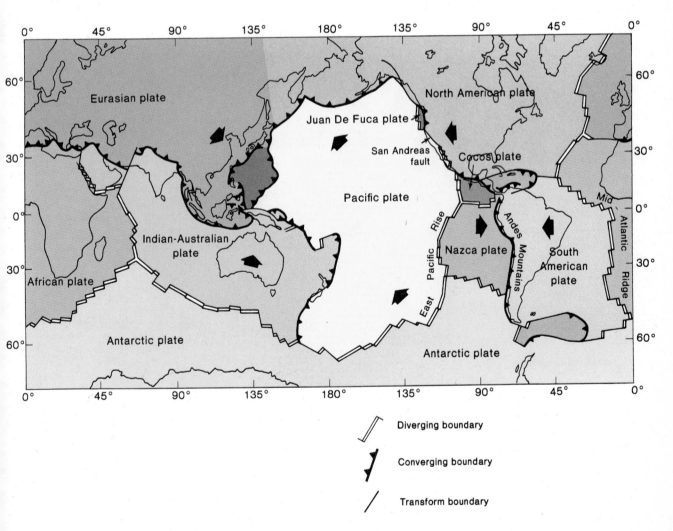

Plates of the World
Figure 1.10

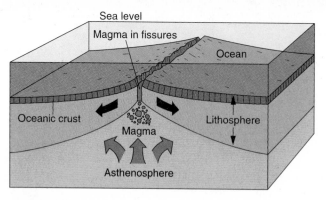

A Divergent Boundary
Figure 1.13

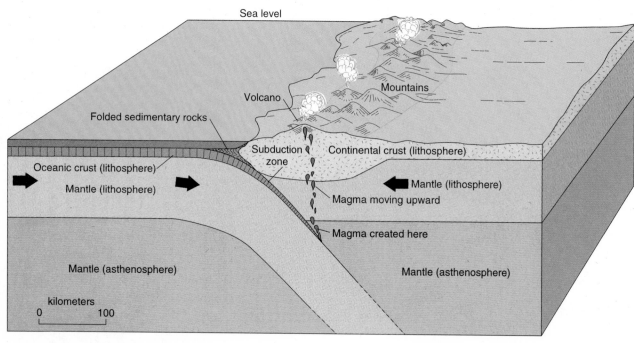

A Convergent Boundary
Figure 1.14

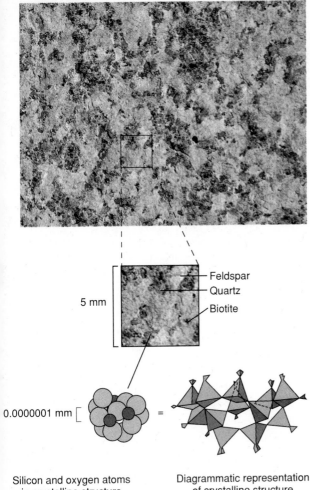

5 mm

Feldspar
Quartz
Biotite

0.0000001 mm

=

Silicon and oxygen atoms
in crystalline structure

Diagrammatic representation
of crystalline structure

Granite: Rock, Mineral and Atomic Structure
Figure 2.1

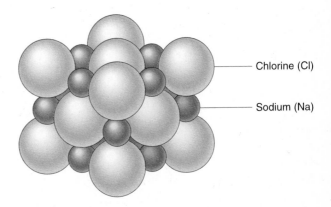

Chlorine (Cl)

Sodium (Na)

Crystal Structure of Halite
Figure 2.2

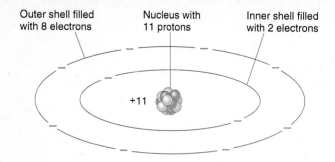

Outer shell filled
with 8 electrons

Nucleus with
11 protons

Inner shell filled
with 2 electrons

+11

A   Sodium (Na⁺)

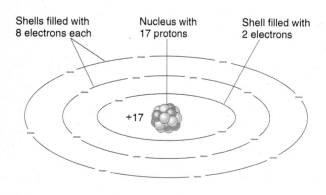

Shells filled with
8 electrons each

Nucleus with
17 protons

Shell filled with
2 electrons

+17

B   Chlorine (Cl⁻)

● Protons   ○ Neutrons   — Electrons

Sodium and Chlorine Ions
Figure 2.5

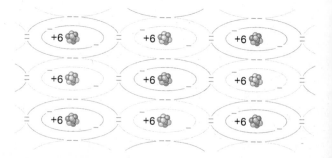

Carbon Atoms in Diamond
Box 2.1;2

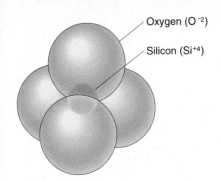

A Arrangement of atoms in
   silica tetrahedron

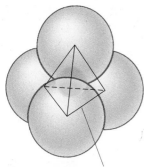

B Diagrammatic representation
   of a silica tetrahedron

Silica Tetrahedron
Figure 2.7

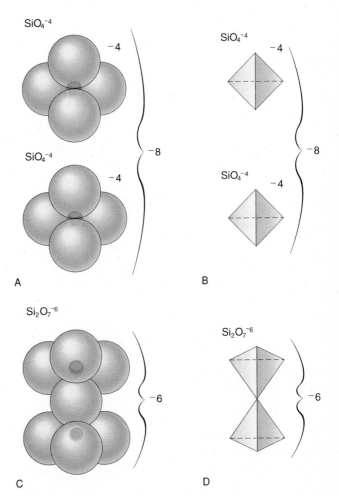

SiO_4^{-4} −4

SiO_4^{-4} −4

} −8

A

SiO_4^{-4} −4

SiO_4^{-4} −4

} −8

B

$Si_2O_7^{-6}$

} −6

C

$Si_2O_7^{-6}$

} −6

D

Silica Tetrahedra Sharing Oxygen Atoms
Figure 2.8

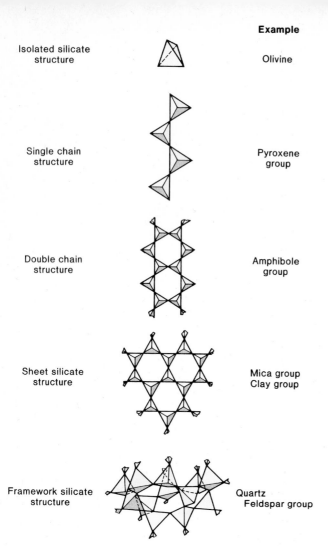

	Example
Isolated silicate structure	Olivine
Single chain structure	Pyroxene group
Double chain structure	Amphibole group
Sheet silicate structure	Mica group Clay group
Framework silicate structure	Quartz Feldspar group

Common Silicate Structures
Figure 2.9

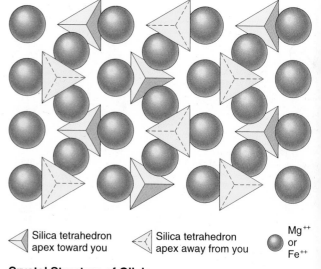

◁ Silica tetrahedron apex toward you   ◁ Silica tetrahedron apex away from you   ● Mg^{++} or Fe^{++}

Crystal Structure of Olivine
Figure 2.10

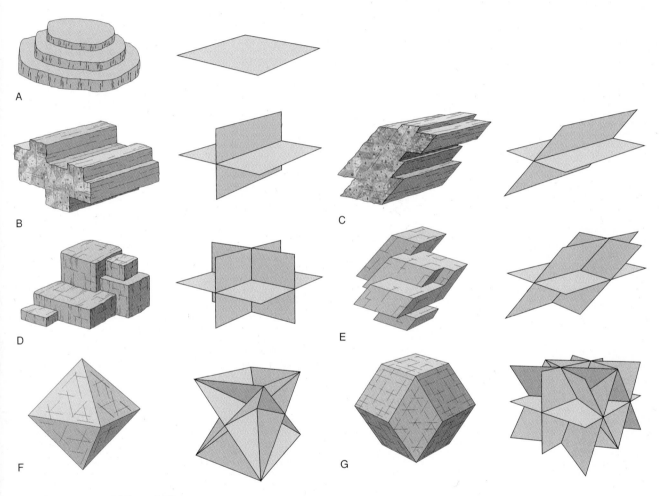

Possible Types of Mineral Cleavage
Figure 2.20

A

B

C

D

E

F

G

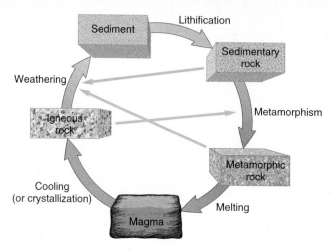

Rock Cycle
Figure 2.27

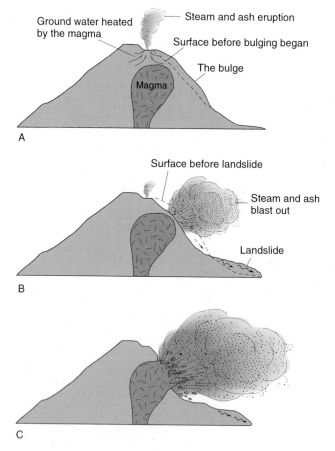

A

B

C

Eruption of Mount St. Helens
Box 3.1;2

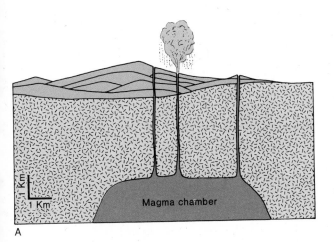

A

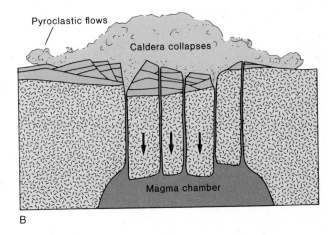

B

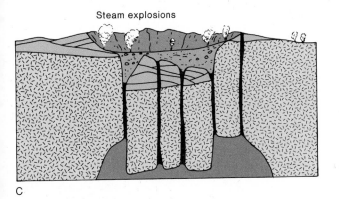

C

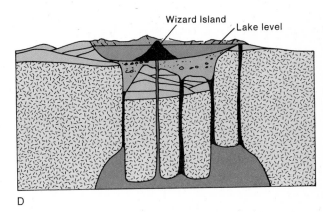

D

Development of Crater Lake
Figure 3.4

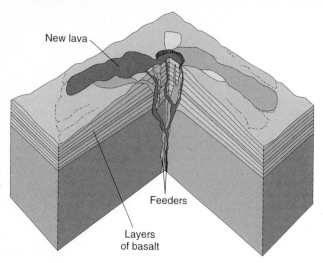

Shield Volcano
Figure 3.16

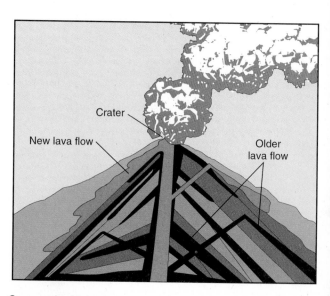

Composite Volcano
Figure 3.22

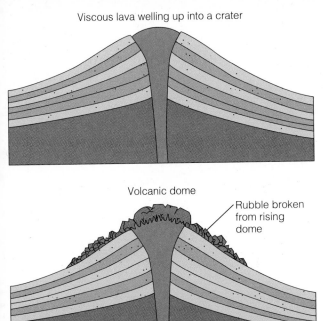

Viscous lava welling up into a crater

Volcanic dome

Rubble broken
from rising
dome

Volcanic Dome within a Cinder Cone
Figure 3.28

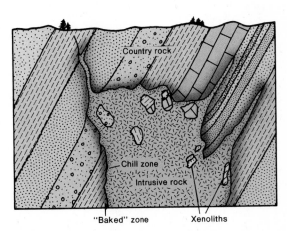

Country rock

Chill zone

Intrusive rock

"Baked" zone   Xenoliths

Igneous Rock Intruding Country Rock
Figure 4.1

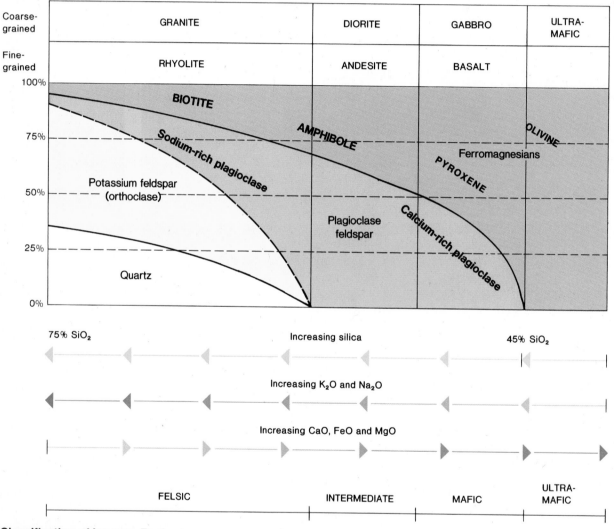

Classification of Igneous Rocks
Figure 4.4

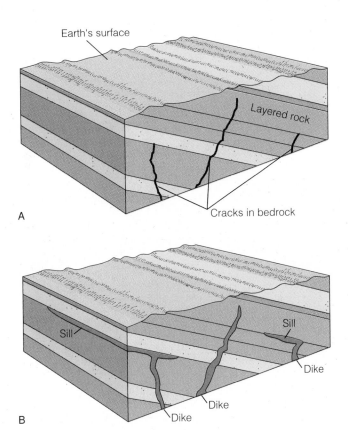

Earth's surface

Layered rock

Cracks in bedrock

A

Sill

Sill

Dike

Dike

Dike

B

Dikes and Sills
Figure 4.7

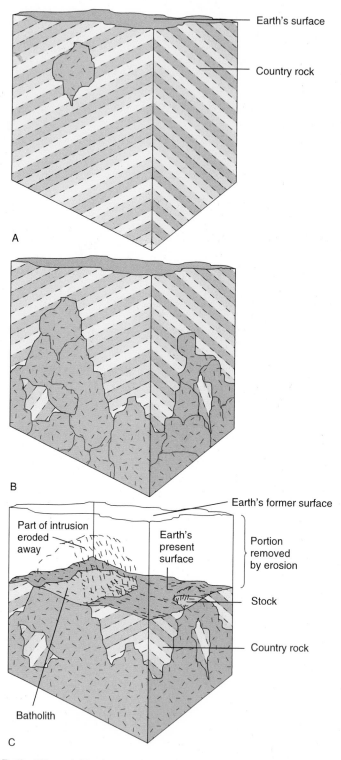

Earth's surface

Country rock

A

B

Earth's former surface

Part of intrusion eroded away

Earth's present surface

Portion removed by erosion

Stock

Country rock

Batholith

C

Batholith and Stock
Figure 4.10

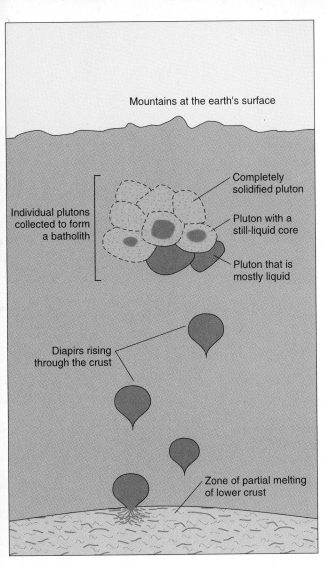

Diapirs of Magma in the Crust
Figure 4.11

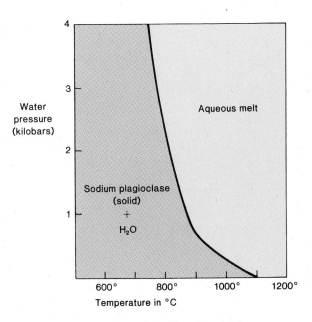

Melting Temperatures of Sodium Plagioclase
Figure 4.14

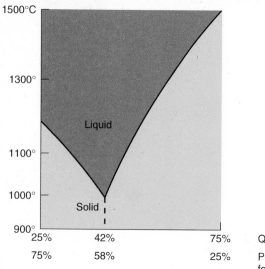

1500°C

1300°

1100°

Liquid

1000°

Solid

900°

| | 25% | 42% | | 75% | Quartz |
| 75% | | 58% | 25% | | Potassium feldspar |

Quartz/Potassium Feldspar Phase Diagram
Figure 4.15

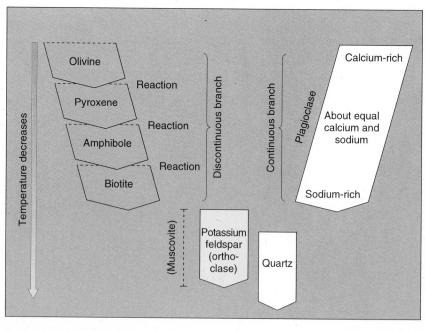

Bowen's Reaction Series
Figure 4.16

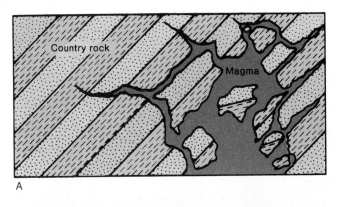

A

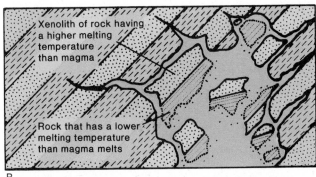

B

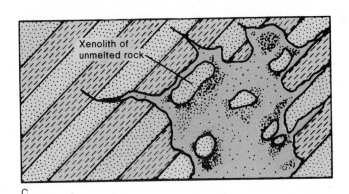

C

Assimilation of Country Rock
Figure 4.18

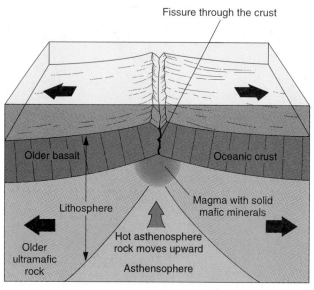

Fissure through the crust

Older basalt

Oceanic crust

Lithosphere

Magma with solid
mafic minerals

Older
ultramafic
rock

Hot asthenosphere
rock moves upward

Asthensophere

A

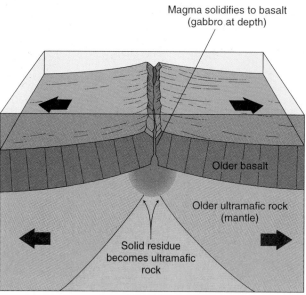

Magma solidifies to basalt
(gabbro at depth)

Older basalt

Older ultramafic rock
(mantle)

Solid residue
becomes ultramafic
rock

B

Formation of Oceanic Crust (Divergent Boundary)
Figure 4.20

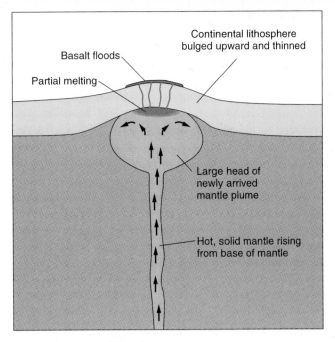

Mantle Plumes and Flood Basalts
Figure 4.21

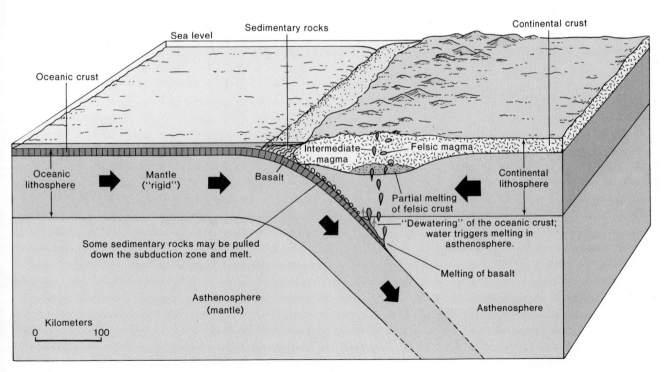

Magma Generation at Convergent Boundary
Figure 4.22

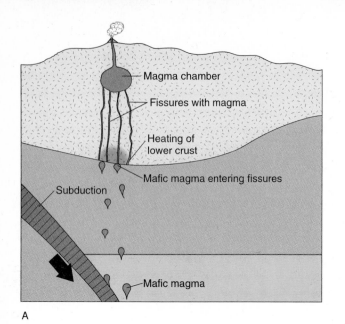

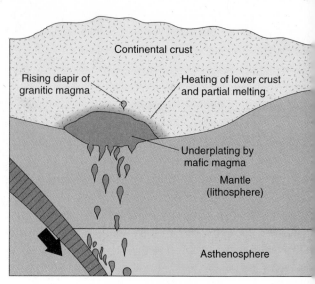

A

B

Mafic Magma Melting Lower Crust
Figure 4.23

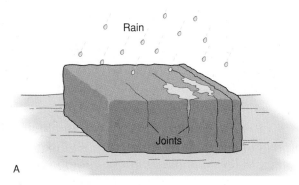

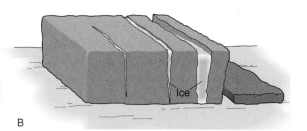

A

B

Frost Wedging
Figure 5.7

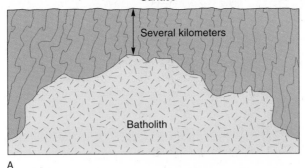

Surface

Several kilometers

Batholith

A

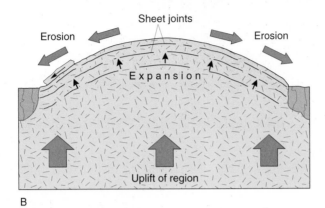

Sheet joints

Erosion

Erosion

Expansion

Uplift of region

B

Exfoliation by Pressure Release
Figure 5.10

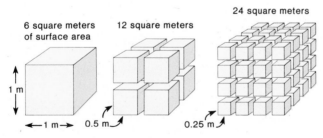

6 square meters
of surface area

12 square meters

24 square meters

1 m

1 m

0.5 m

0.25 m

Mechanical Weathering and Surface Area Increase
Figure 5.14

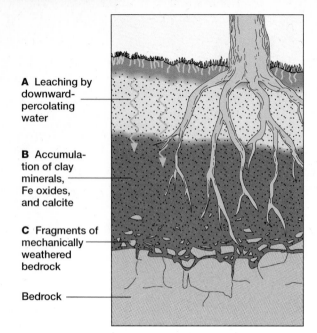

A Leaching by downward-percolating water

B Accumulation of clay minerals, Fe oxides, and calcite

C Fragments of mechanically weathered bedrock

Bedrock

A

Soil Horizons
Figure 5.20a

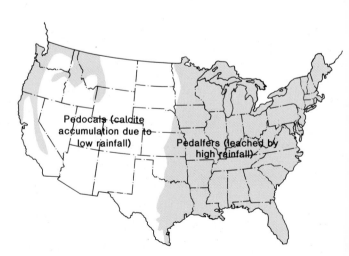

Pedocals (calcite accumulation due to low rainfall)

Pedalfers (leached by high rainfall)

Pedalfer and Pedocal Soils in U.S.
Figure 5.22

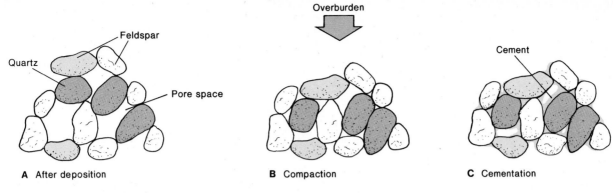

Lithification of Sand Grains
Figure 6.6

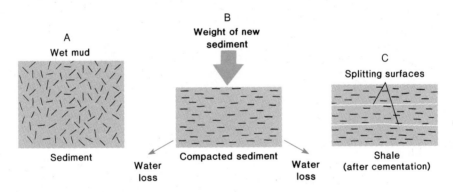

Lithification of Muddy Sediment
Figure 6.15

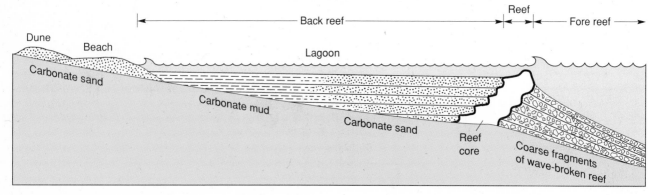

Cross Section of a Coral Reef
Figure 6.18

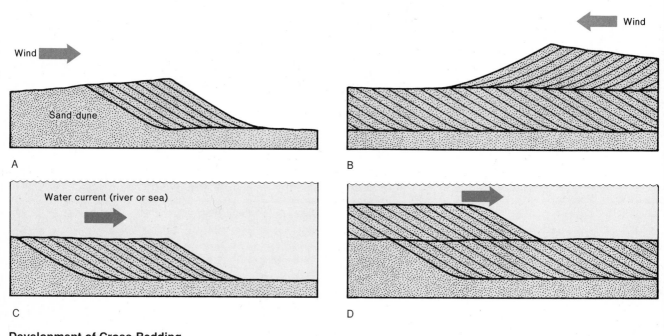

A

B

C

D

Development of Cross-Bedding
Figure 6.28

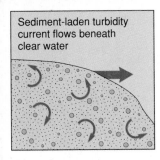

Sediment-laden turbidity current flows beneath clear water

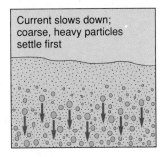

Current slows down; coarse, heavy particles settle first

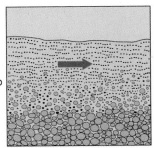

Main body of current comes to rest

Fine-grained "tail" of turbidity current continues to flow, adding fine-grained sediment to top of deposit

Progressively finer sediments settle on top of coarse particles

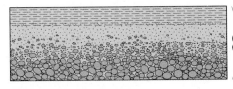

A graded bed

Development of a Graded Bed
Figure 6.30

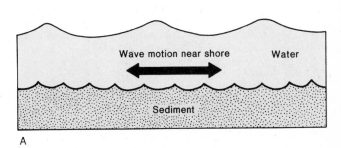

Wave motion near shore

Water

Sediment

A

Current (water or wind)

Sediment

B

Development of Ripple Marks
Figure 6.32

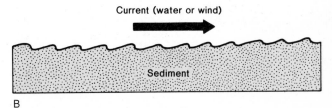

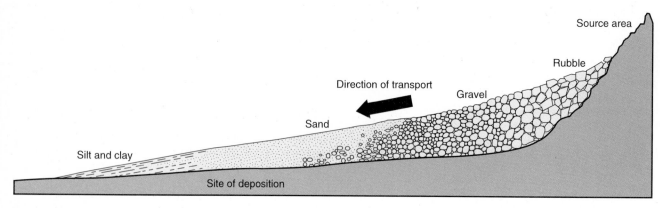

Sediment Thickness/Coarseness and Source Area
Figure 6.37

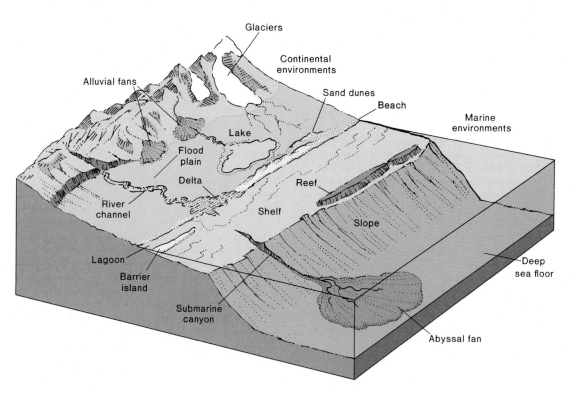

Sedimentary Depositional Environments
Figure 6.39

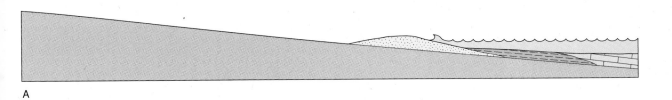

A

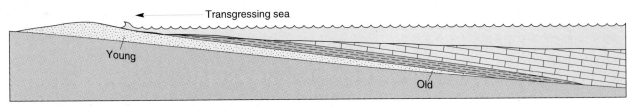

Transgressing sea

Young

Old

B   Transgression — rising sea level or subsiding land

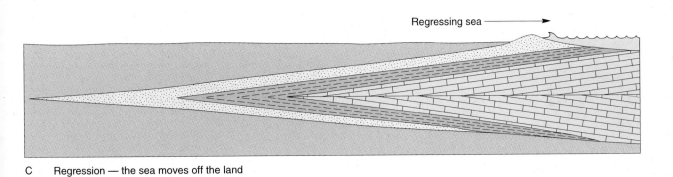

Regressing sea

C   Regression — the sea moves off the land

Sea Transgressions and Regressions
Box 6.2;1

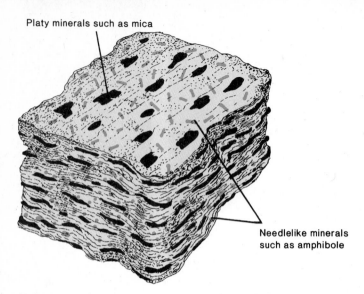

Platy minerals such as mica

Needlelike minerals
such as amphibole

Schistose Texture
Figure 7.6

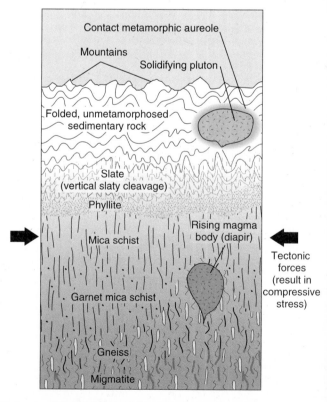

Contact metamorphic aureole

Mountains

Solidifying pluton

Folded, unmetamorphosed
sedimentary rock

Slate
(vertical slaty cleavage)

Phyllite

Mica schist

Rising magma
body (diapir)

Garnet mica schist

Tectonic
forces
(result in
compressive
stress)

Gneiss

Migmatite

Metamorphism in Upper Crust
Figure 7.9

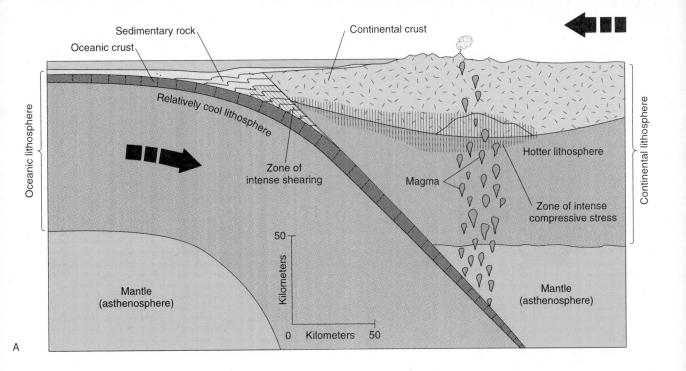

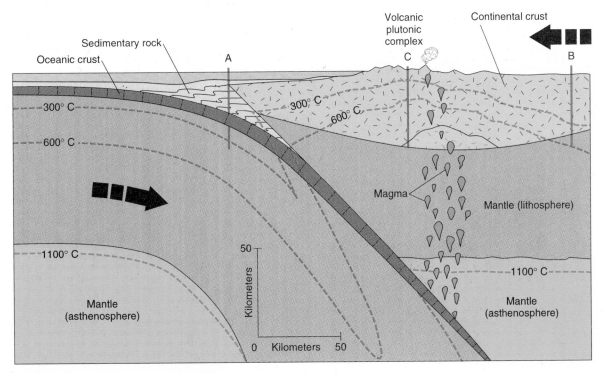

Metamorphism at a Convergent Boundary
Figure 7.16

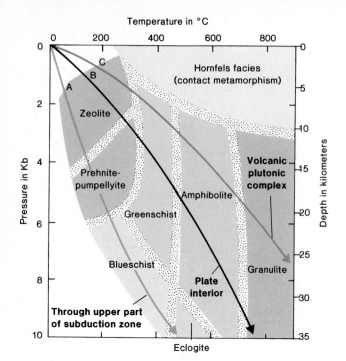

Temperature in °C

Hornfels facies
(contact metamorphism)

Zeolite

Prehnite-
pumpellyite

Amphibolite

Greenschist

**Volcanic
plutonic
complex**

Blueschist

Granulite

**Plate
interior**

**Through upper part
of subduction zone**

Eclogite

Metamorphic Facies
Box 7.3;1

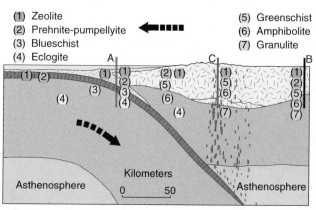

(1) Zeolite   (5) Greenschist
(2) Prehnite-pumpellyite   (6) Amphibolite
(3) Blueschist   (7) Granulite
(4) Eclogite

Asthenosphere   Kilometers   Asthenosphere

0   50

Metamorphic Facies at a Convergent Boundary
Box 7.3;2

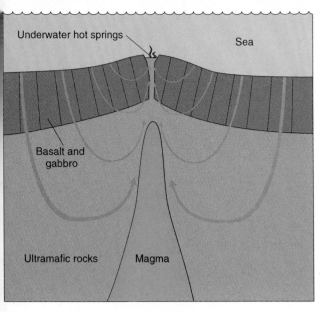

Hydrothermal Activity at Mid-Ocean Ridge
Figure 7.17

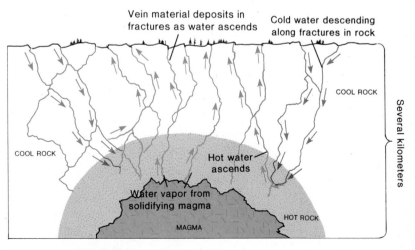

Formation of Hydrothermal Veins
Figure 7.20

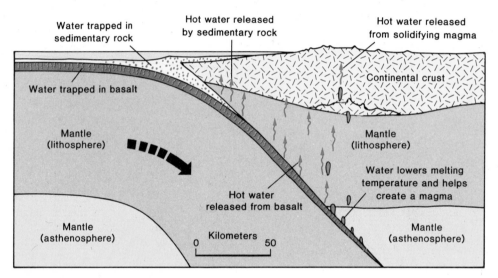

Movement of Water at Convergent Boundary
Figure 7.21

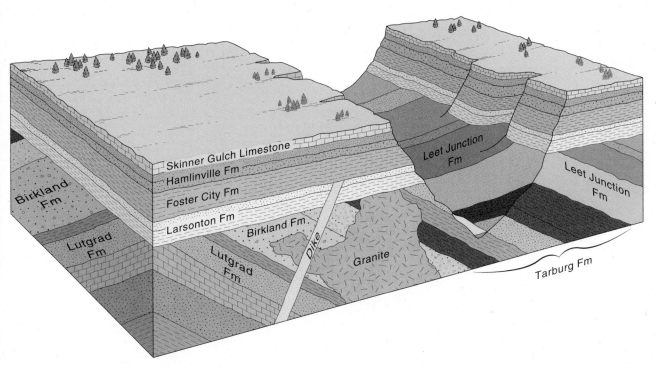

Skinner Gulch Limestone
Hamlinville Fm
Foster City Fm
Larsonton Fm
Birkland Fm
Birkland Fm
Lutgrad Fm
Lutgrad Fm
Dike
Granite
Leet Junction Fm
Leet Junction Fm
Tarburg Fm

Block Diagram of Miner Canyon
Figure 8.1

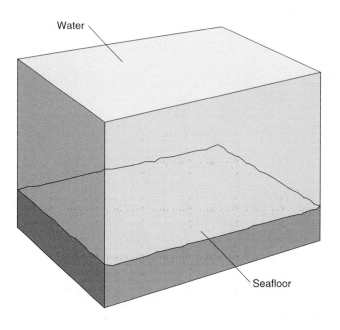

Water

Seafloor

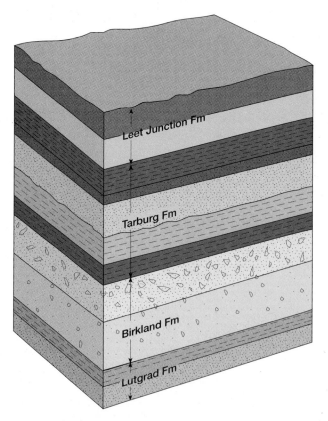

Leet Junction Fm

Tarburg Fm

Birkland Fm

Lutgrad Fm

Geologic Evolution of Miner Canyon
Figure 8.2 & 8.3

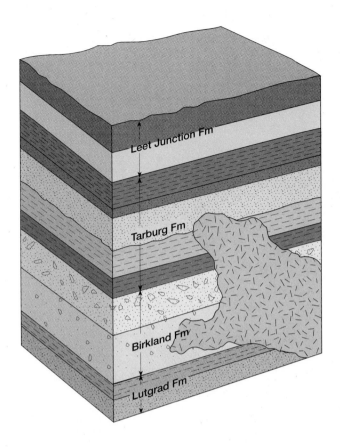

Leet Junction Fm

Tarburg Fm

Birkland Fm

Lutgrad Fm

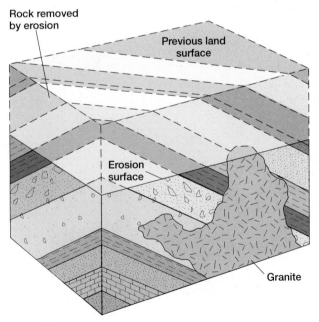

Rock removed
by erosion

Previous land
surface

Erosion
surface

Granite

Geologic Evolution of Miner Canyon
Figure 8.4 & 8.5

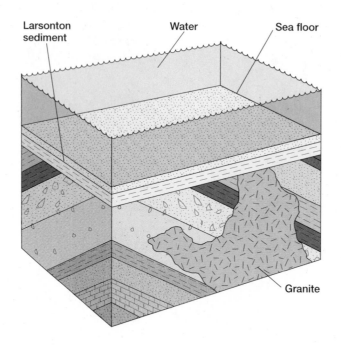

Larsonton sediment

Water

Sea floor

Granite

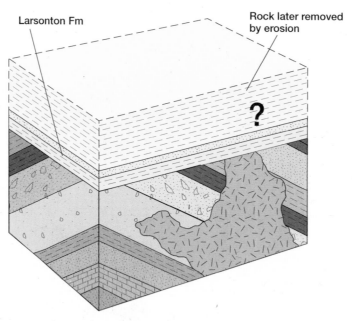

Larsonton Fm

Rock later removed by erosion

?

Geologic Evolution of Miner Canyon
Figure 8.6 & 8.7

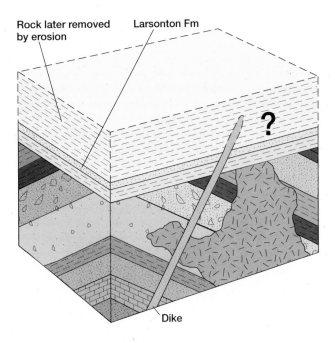

Rock later removed by erosion

Larsonton Fm

?

Dike

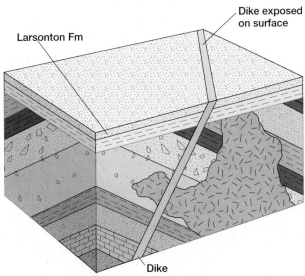

Larsonton Fm

Dike exposed on surface

Dike

Geologic Evolution of Miner Canyon
Figure 8.8 & 8.9

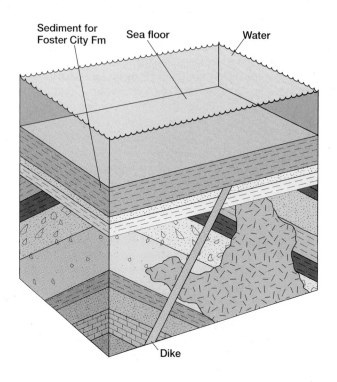

Sediment for Foster City Fm

Sea floor

Water

Dike

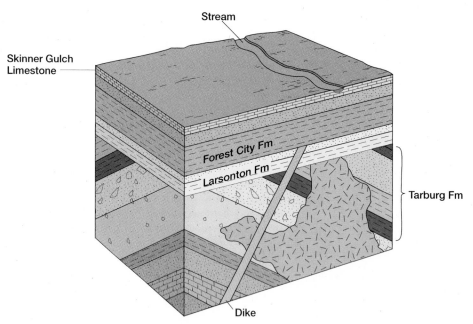

Stream

Skinner Gulch Limestone

Forest City Fm

Larsonton Fm

Tarburg Fm

Dike

Geologic Evolution of Miner Canyon
Figure 8.10 & 8.11

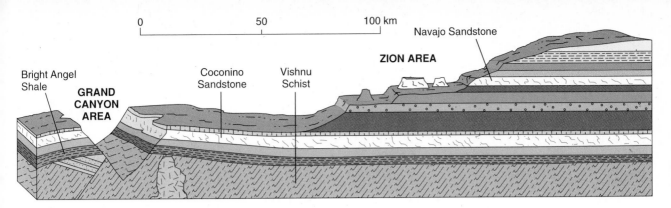

Cross Section Through Colorado Plateau
Figure 8.14

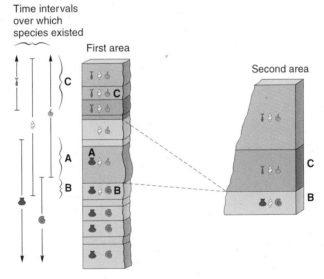

Relative Ages by Using Fossil Assemblages
Figure 8.15

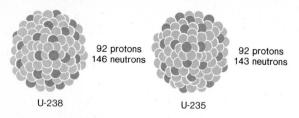

92 protons
146 neutrons

92 protons
143 neutrons

U-238

U-235

Uranium Isotopes
Figure 8.17

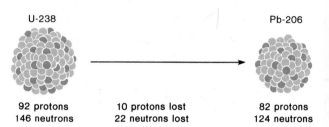

U-238

Pb-206

92 protons
146 neutrons

10 protons lost
22 neutrons lost

82 protons
124 neutrons

Decay of Uranium-238 to Lead-206
Figure 8.18

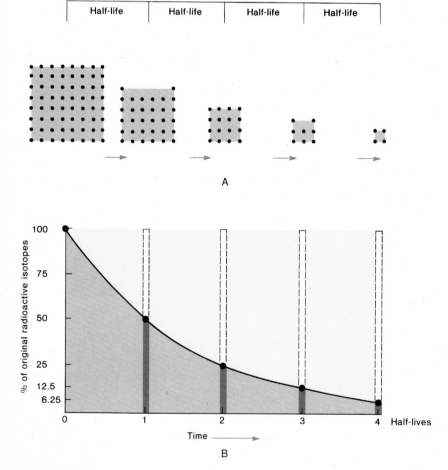

Half-Life Diagram
Figure 8.19

EON	ERA	PERIOD	EPOCH	Approximate Age in Millions of Years Before Present		
Phanerozoic	Cenozoic	Quaternary	Recent (Holocene)	.01		
			Pleistocene	1.6		
		Tertiary	Pliocene	5.3		
			Miocene	23.7		
			Oligocene	36.6		
			Eocene	57.8		
			Paleocene	66.4		
	Mesozoic	Cretaceous		144		
		Jurassic		208		
		Triassic		245		
	Paleozoic	Permian		286		
		Pennsylvanian		320		
		Mississippian		360		
		Devonian		408		
		Silurian		438		
		Ordovician		505		
		Cambrian		545		
Proterozoic		PRECAMBRIAN		2,500		
Archean						
		Origin of earth		4,500		

Geologic Time Scale
Figure 8.21

Time Whorl
Figure 8.22

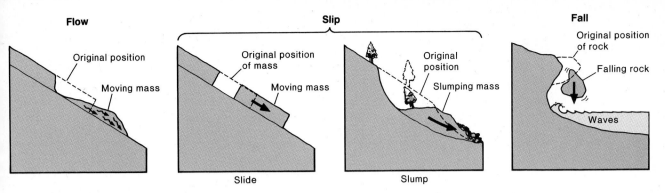

Mass Wasting: Flow, Slip and Fall
Figure 9.1

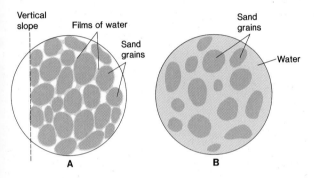

Effect of Water in Sand
Figure 9.3

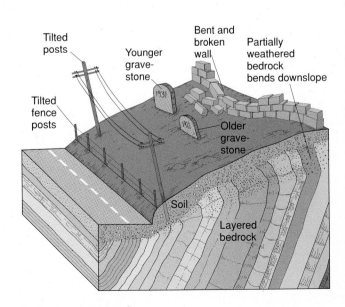

Indicators of Creep
Figure 9.4

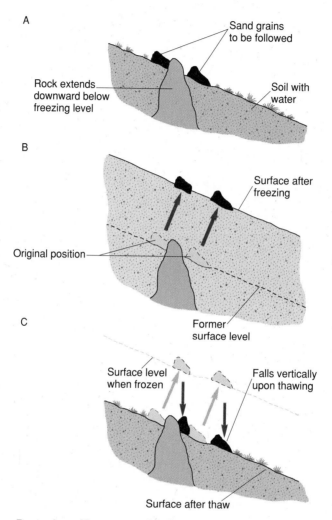

A

Sand grains to be followed

Rock extends downward below freezing level

Soil with water

B

Surface after freezing

Original position

Former surface level

C

Surface level when frozen

Falls vertically upon thawing

Surface after thaw

Downslope Movement of Soil
Figure 9.6

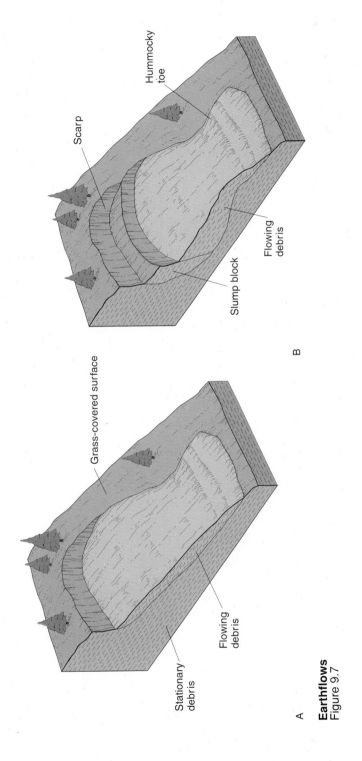

Earthflows
Figure 9.7

A

Stationary debris

Grass-covered surface

Flowing debris

B

Scarp

Hummocky toe

Slump block

Flowing debris

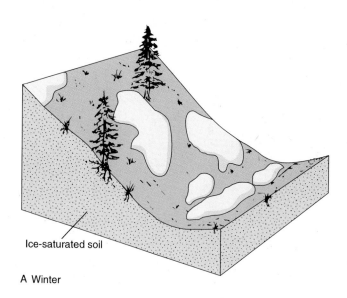

Ice-saturated soil

A Winter

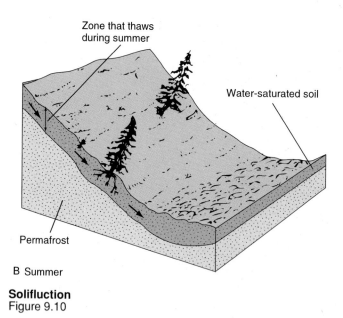

Zone that thaws
during summer

Water-saturated soil

Permafrost

B Summer

Solifluction
Figure 9.10

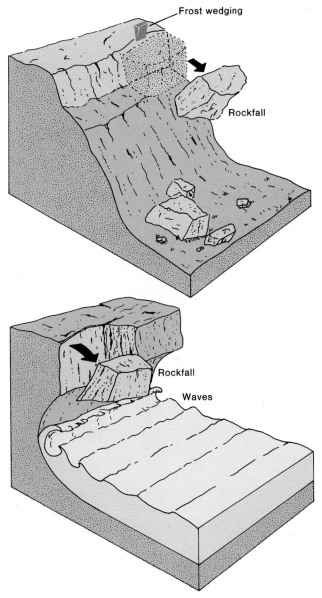

Rock Falls
Figure 9.14

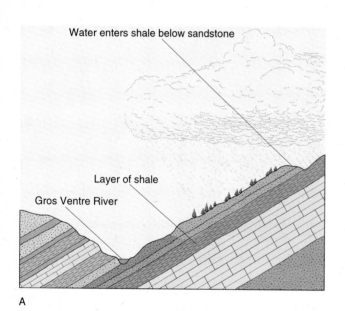

Water enters shale below sandstone

Layer of shale

Gros Ventre River

A

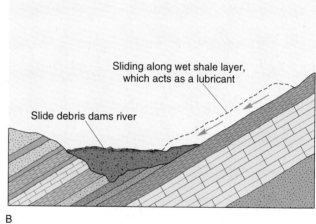

Sliding along wet shale layer, which acts as a lubricant

Slide debris dams river

B

Diagram of the Gros Ventre Slide
Figure 9.16a-b

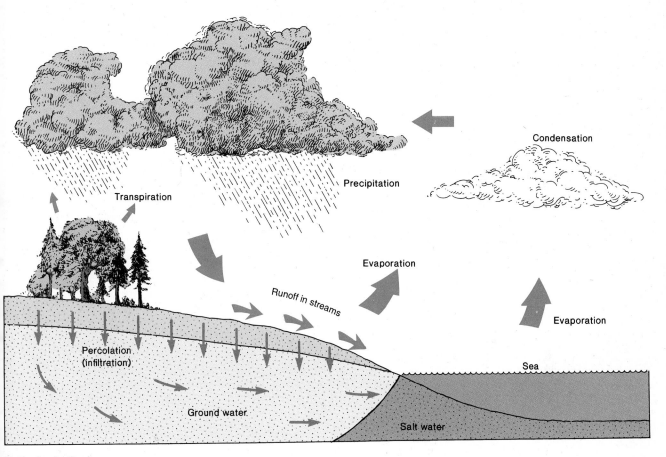

Condensation

Precipitation

Transpiration

Evaporation

Runoff in streams

Evaporation

Percolation
(infiltration)

Sea

Ground water

Salt water

Hydrologic Cycle
Figure 10.1

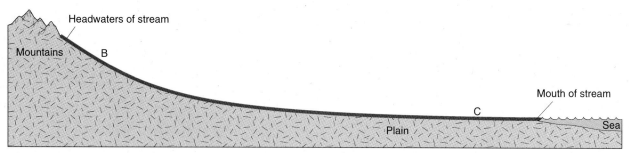

A   Longitudinal profile (dark blue line) of a stream beginning in mountains and flowing across a plain into the sea.

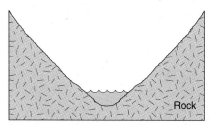

B   Cross profile of the stream at point B. The channel is at the bottom of a V-shaped valley cut into rock.

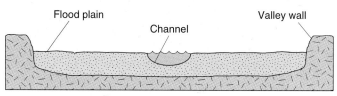

C   Cross profile at point C. The channel is surrounded by a broad flood plain of sediment.

Longitudinal and Cross Profiles of a Stream
Figure 10.2

Drainage Basin of Mississippi River
Figure 10.4

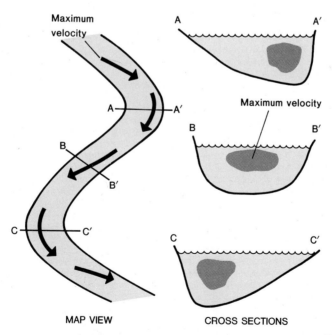

MAP VIEW   CROSS SECTIONS

Maximum Velocity Regions in a Stream
Figure 10.12

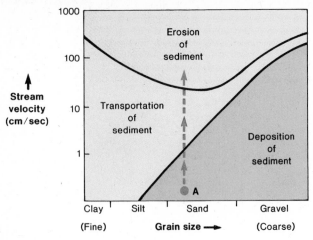

Stream Velocity and Sediment Erosion/Deposition
Figure 10.13

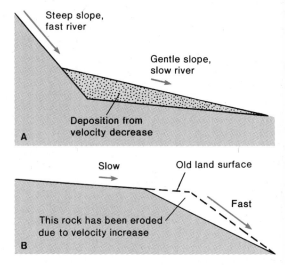

Changes in Stream Gradient
Figure 10.14

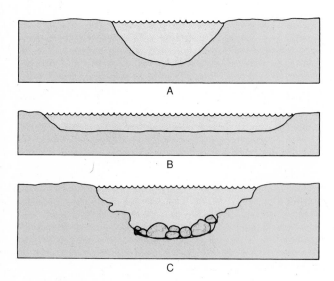

Channel Shape and Roughness
Figure 10.17

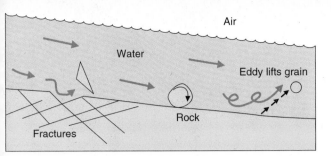

Hydraulic Action
Figure 10.20

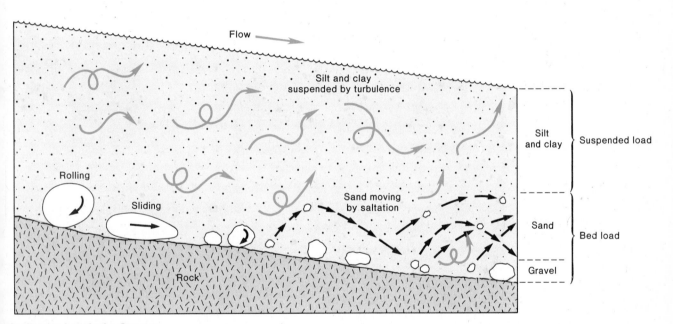

Sediment Load of a Stream
Figure 10.23

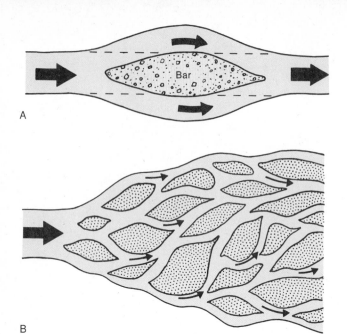

A

B

Mid-Channel Bars and Braided Stream
Figure 10.26

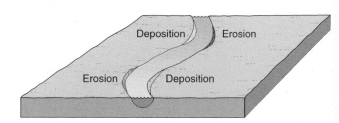

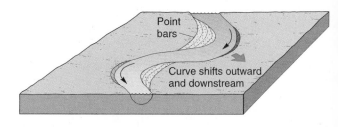

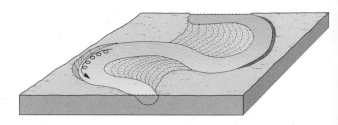

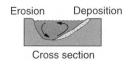

Cross section

Corkscrew water motion on a curve helps cause erosion and deposition.

Development of Meanders and Point Bars
Figure 10.30a

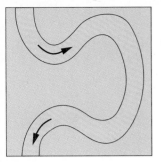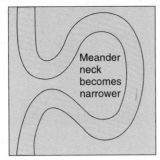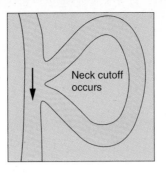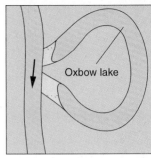

Meander neck becomes narrower

Neck cutoff occurs

Oxbow lake

Creation of Oxbow Lake
Figure 10.31

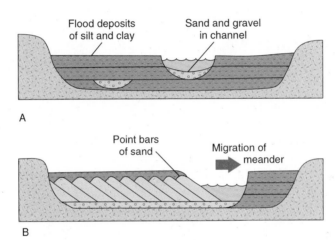

Flood deposits of silt and clay

Sand and gravel in channel

A

Point bars of sand

Migration of meander

B

Flood Plains
Figure 10.35

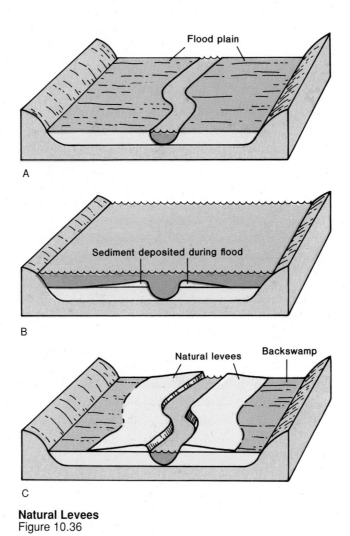

Natural Levees
Figure 10.36

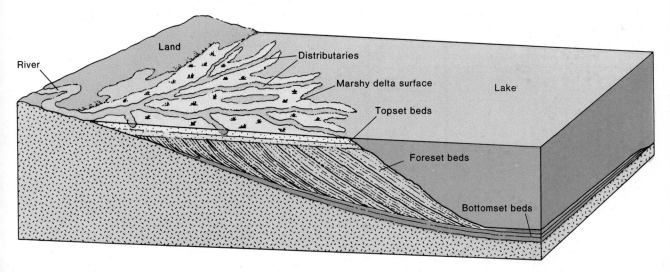

River

Land

Distributaries

Marshy delta surface

Lake

Topset beds

Foreset beds

Bottomset beds

Internal Construction of Small Delta
Figure 10.38

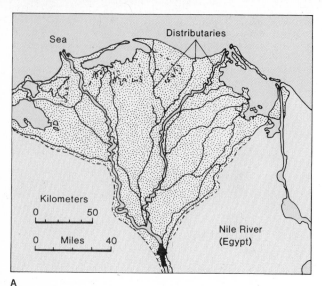

A

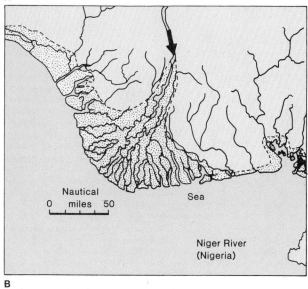

B

Deltas: Nile River and Niger River
Figure 10.39a,b

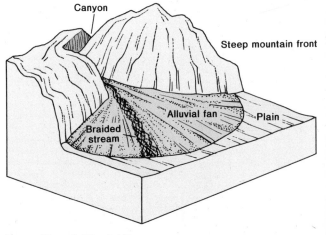

Formation of Alluvial Fan
Figure 10.40

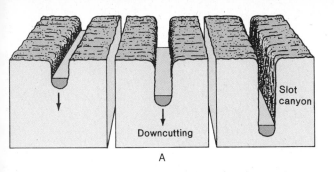

A

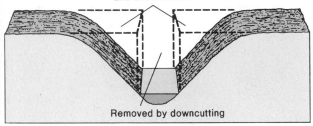

B

Canyons and Valleys
Figure 10.42

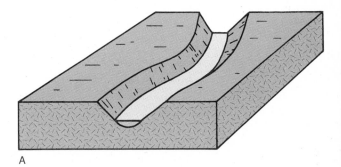

A

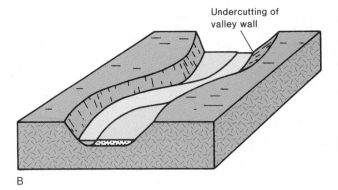

B

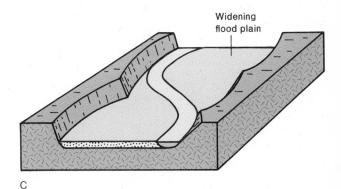

C

Widening of a Stream Valley
Figure 10.47

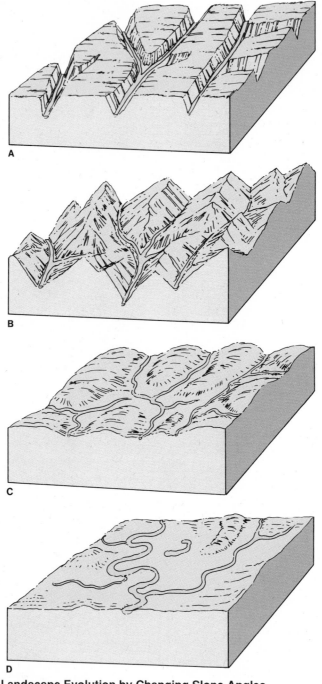

A

B

C

D

Landscape Evolution by Changing Slope Angles
Figure 10.49

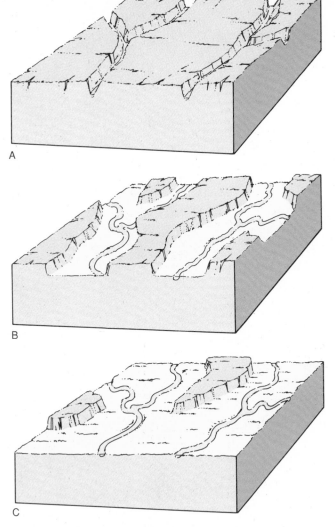

Landscape Evolution by Constant Slope Angle
Figure 10.50

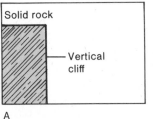

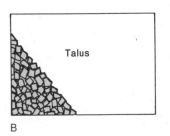

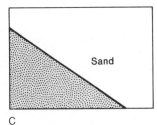

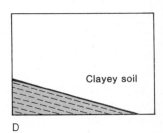

Maximum Slope Angles
Figure 10.51

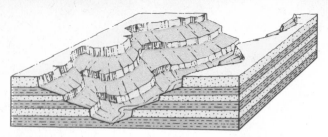

Differential Erosion Producing Cliffs and Slopes
Figure 10.52

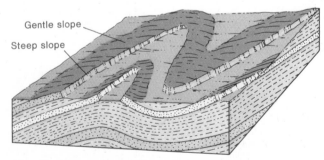

Gentle slope

Steep slope

Erosion of Folded Sedimentary Rocks
Figure 10.53

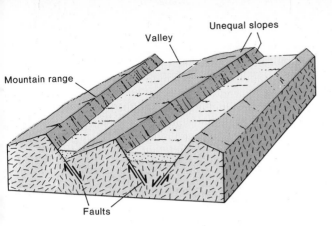

Fault Movement Forming Valleys and Ranges
Figure 10.54

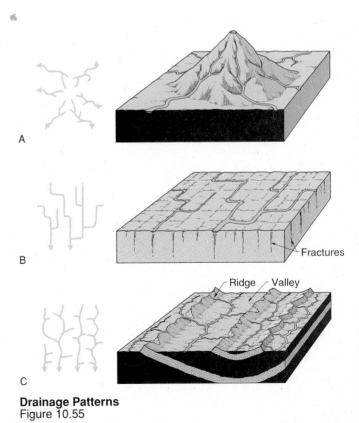

Drainage Patterns
Figure 10.55

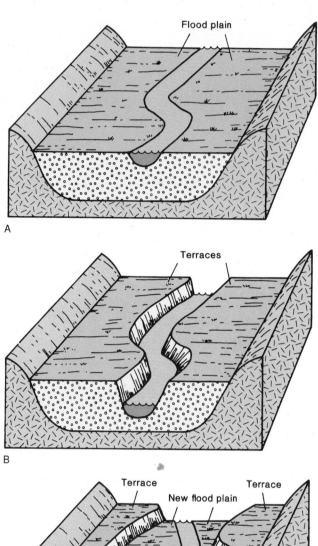

Formation of Stream Terraces
Figure 10.57

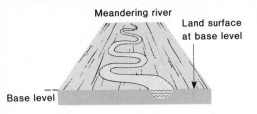

Incised Meanders
Figure 10.60b

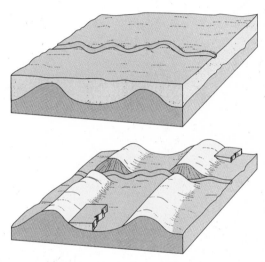

Superimposed Stream
Box 10.2;2a

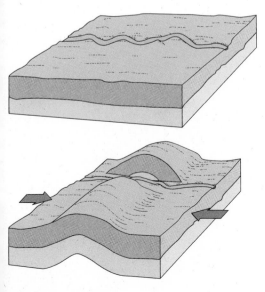

Antecedent Stream
Box 10.2;2b

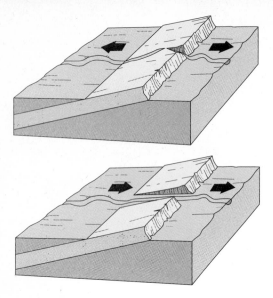

Stream Piracy
Box 10.2;2c

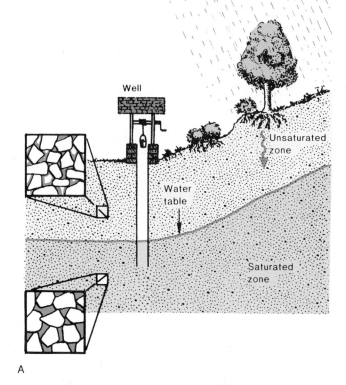

A

Water Table
Figure 11.1a

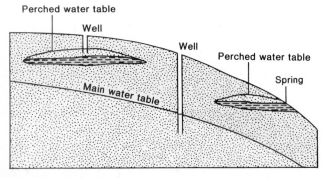

Perched Water Tables
Figure 11.2

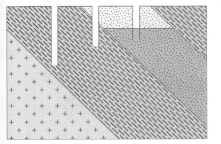

Wells in Sedimentary Rocks
Figure 11.4

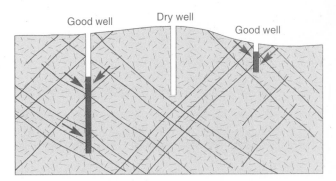

Wells in Crystalline Rock
Figure 11.5

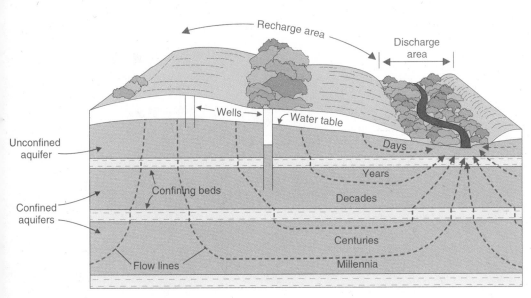

Confined and Unconfined Aquifers
Figure 11.6

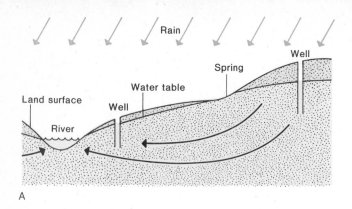

Seasonal Variations in Water Table
Figure 11.7

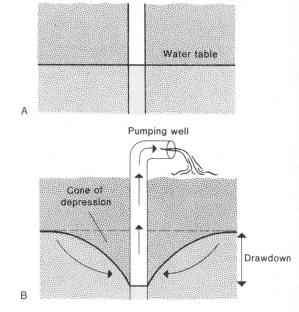

Pumping Well and Cone of Depression
Figure 11.8

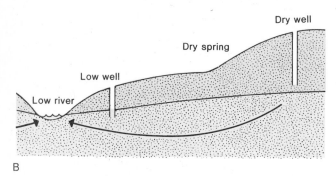

Dakota Sandstone Aquifer
Figure 11.9

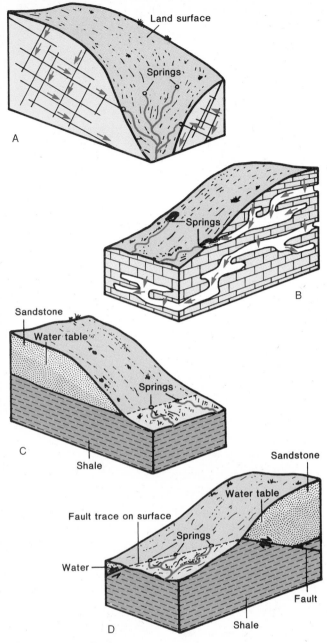

A

B

Sandstone
Water table
Springs

C

Shale

Sandstone
Water table
Fault trace on surface
Springs
Water
Fault
D
Shale

Some Types of Springs
Figure 11.12

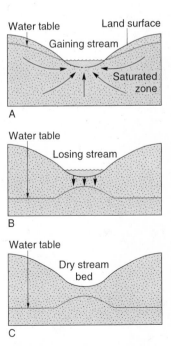

Water table   Land surface
Gaining stream
Saturated
zone
A

Water table
Losing stream
B

Water table
Dry stream
bed
C

Gaining and Losing Streams
Figure 11.13

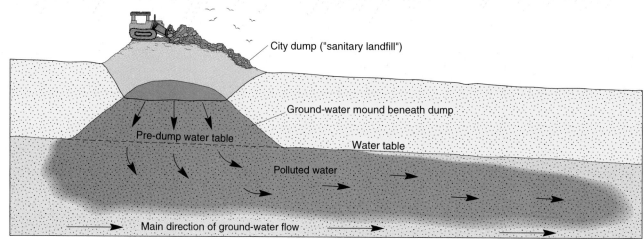

Rain

City dump ("sanitary landfill")

Ground-water mound beneath dump

Pre-dump water table

Water table

Polluted water

Main direction of ground-water flow

A Cross section

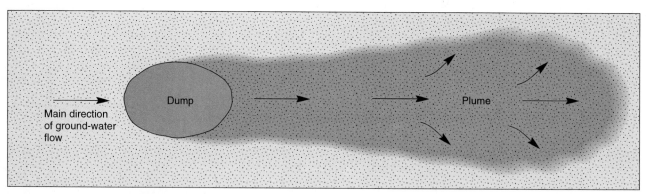

Main direction
of ground-water
flow

Dump

Plume

B Map view of contaminant plume. Note how it grows in size with
   distance from the pollution source.

Contaminant Plume from a Landfill
Figure 11.15

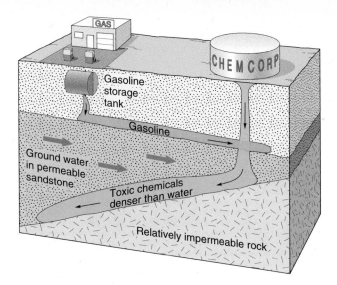

Dense Plume of Toxic Chemicals
Figure 11.16

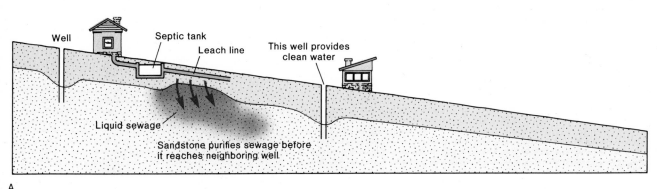

A

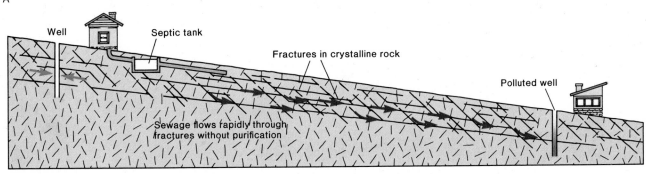

B

Sewage Contamination of Water Wells
Figure 11.17

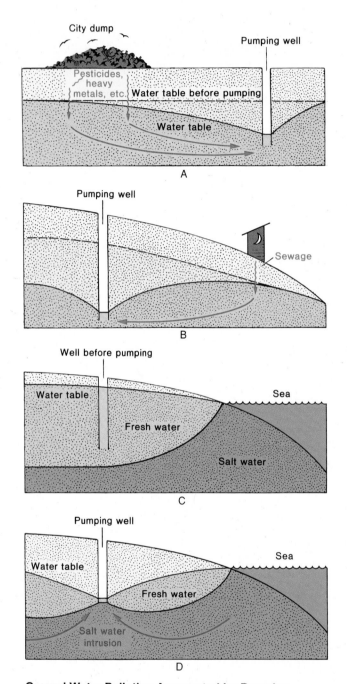

Ground Water Pollution Aggravated by Pumping
Figure 11.18

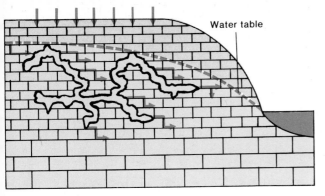

Formation of Caves
Figure 11.20

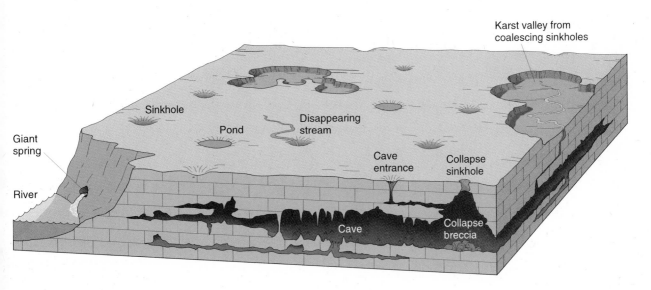

Karst Topography
Figure 11.23

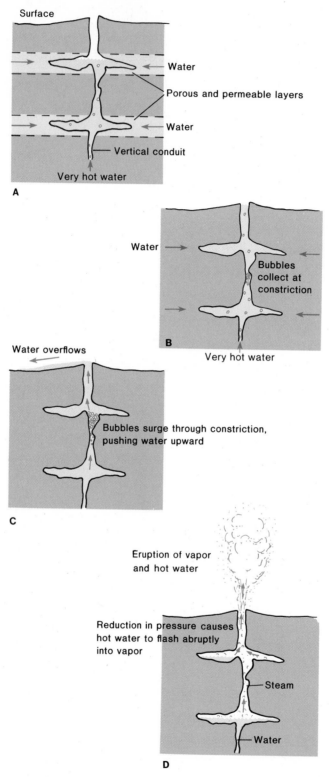

Eruption of a Geyser
Figure 11.27

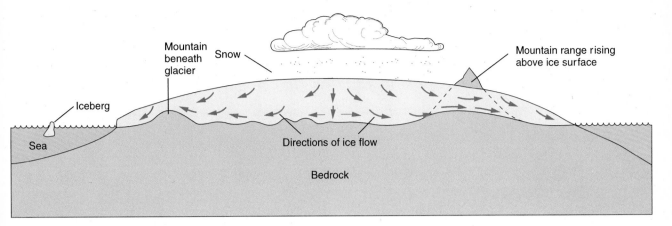

Cross Section of an Ice Sheet
Figure 12.3

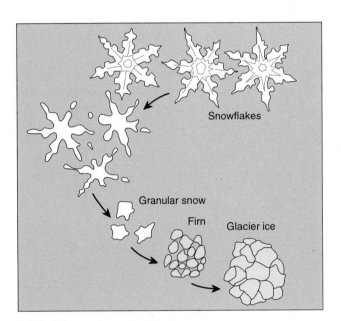

Conversion of Snow to Glacial Ice
Figure 12.4a

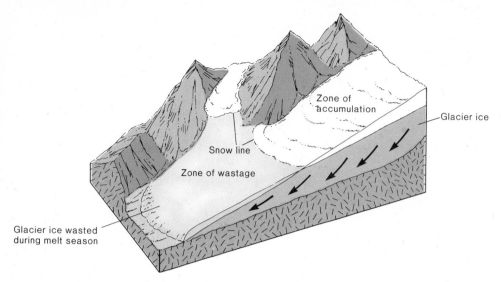

Budget of a Valley Glacier
Figure 12.6

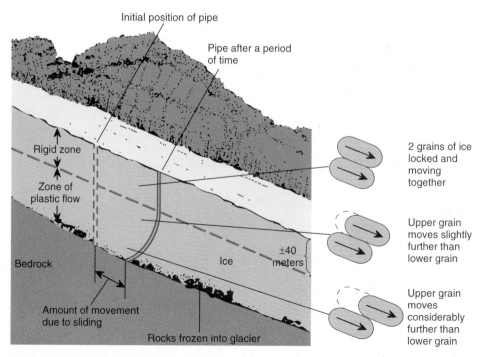

Movement of a Valley Glacier
Figure 12.8

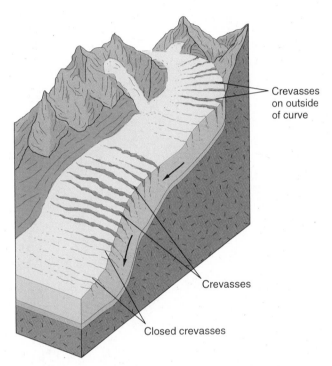

Crevasses
on outside
of curve

Crevasses

Closed crevasses

Formation of Crevasses
Figure 12.10

Map of Antarctica and its Icesheets
Figure 12.12

Ice-surface contour interval 100 meters

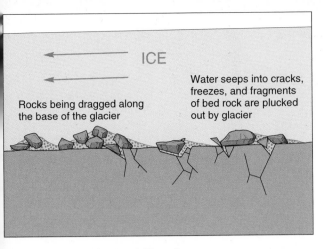

Erosion by Plucking and Abrasion
Figure 12.14

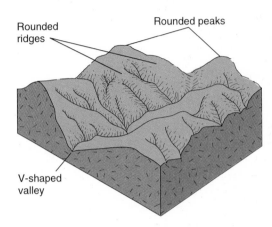

Rounded
ridges

Rounded peaks

V-shaped
valley

A

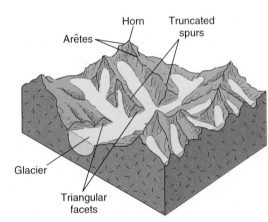

Horn

Truncated
spurs

Arêtes

Glacier

Triangular
facets

B

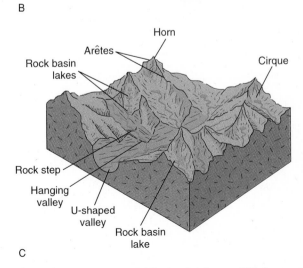

Horn

Arêtes

Cirque

Rock basin
lakes

Rock step

Hanging
valley

U-shaped
valley

Rock basin
lake

C

Mountain Landscape Evolution by Ice and Water
Figure 12.16

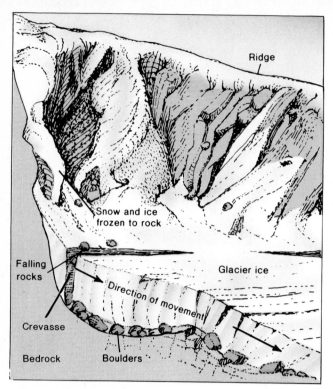

Cutaway View of a Cirque
Figure 12.20b

Labels in figure: Ridge, Snow and ice frozen to rock, Glacier ice, Falling rocks, Direction of movement, Crevasse, Bedrock, Boulders

Moraines Associated with Valley Glaciers
Figure 12.25

Labels in figure: Lateral moraines, Medial moraines, End moraines, Terminus of glacier, Recessional moraine, Ground moraine, Terminal moraine

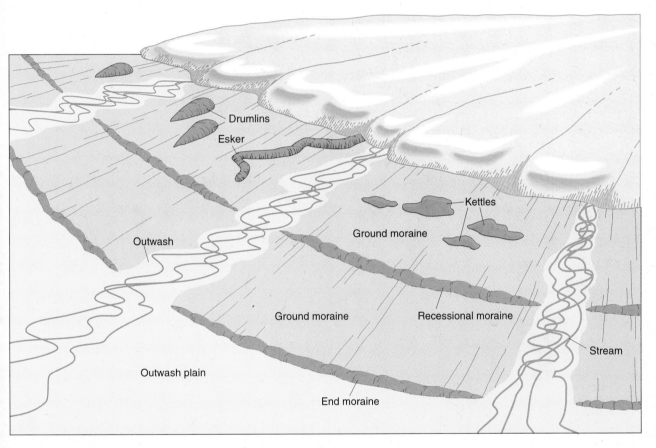

Depositional Features of a Receding Ice Sheet
Figure 12.28

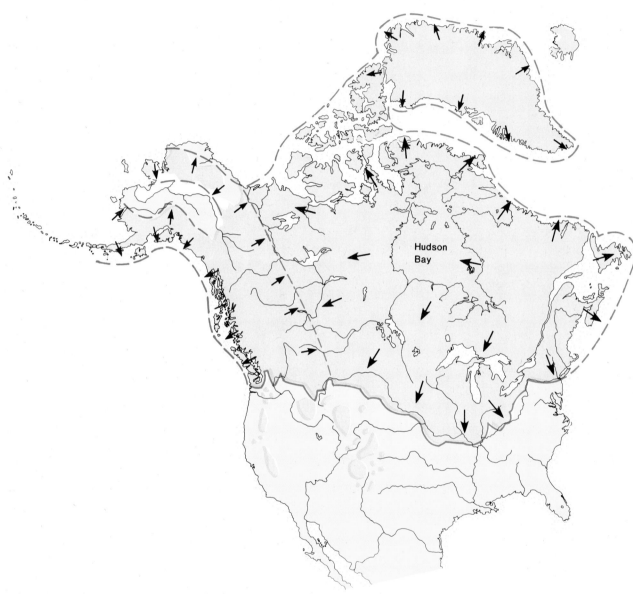

Hudson
Bay

Extent of Pleistocene Glaciation
Figure 12.33

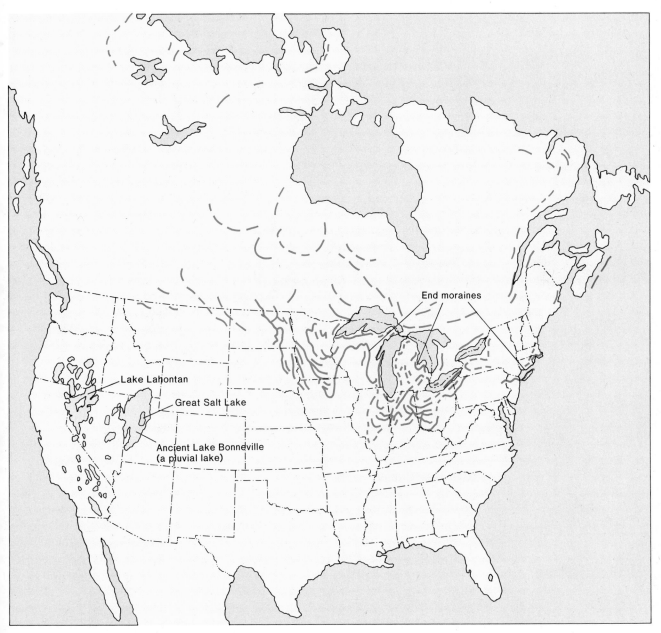

End Moraines in United States and Canada
Figure 12.34

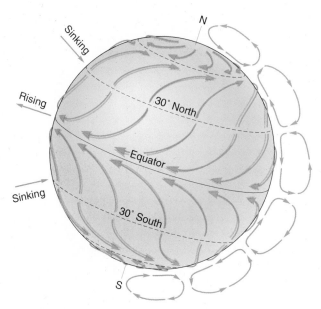

Global Air Circulation
Figure 13.2

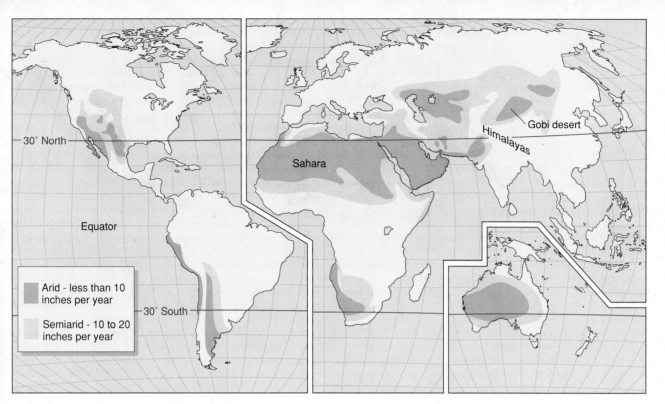

World Distribution of Nonpolar Deserts
Figure 13.3

Legend:
- Arid - less than 10 inches per year
- Semiarid - 10 to 20 inches per year

30° North

Equator

30° South

Sahara

Himalayas

Gobi desert

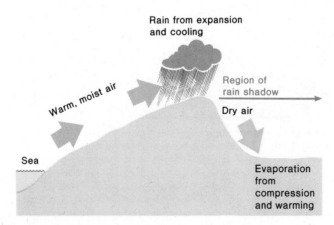

Rainshadow Causing a Desert
Figure 13.4

Rain from expansion and cooling

Warm, moist air

Region of rain shadow

Dry air

Sea

Evaporation from compression and warming

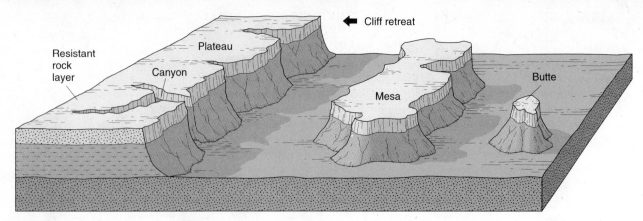

Landforms of the Colorado Plateau
Figure 13.7a

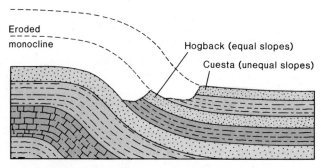

Erosion of a Monocline
Figure 13.8a

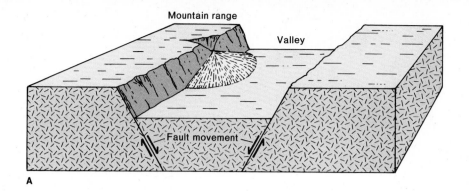

A

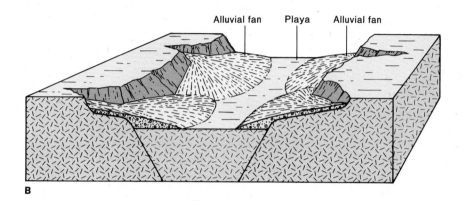

B

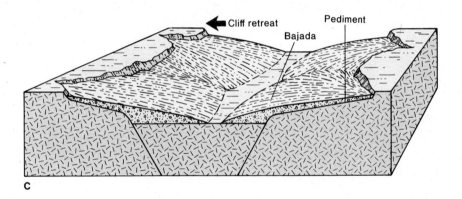

C

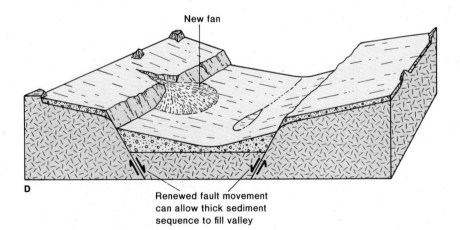

D

Origin of Basin and Range Topography
Figure 13.11

91

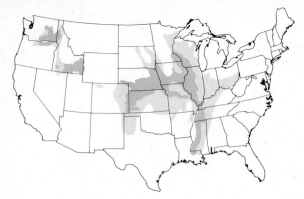

Loess Deposits in the U.S.
Figure 13.20

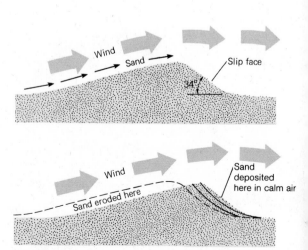

Migration of a Sand Dune
Figure 13.22a

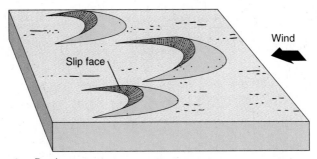

A   Barchans

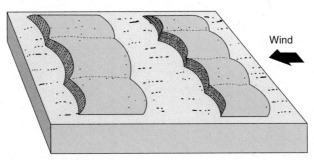

B   Transverse dunes

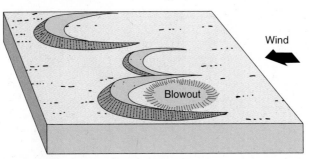

C   Parabolic dunes

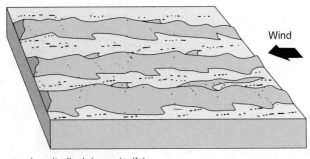

D   Longitudinal dunes (seifs)

Types of Sand Dunes
Figure 13.24

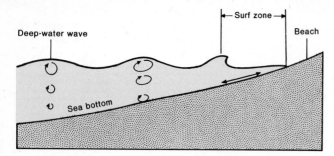

Deep Water Waves and the Surf Zone
Figure 14.4

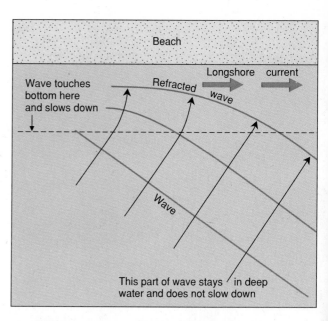

Wave Refraction Along Straight Coast
Figure 14.6

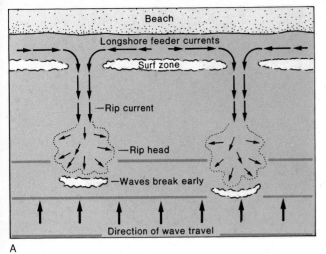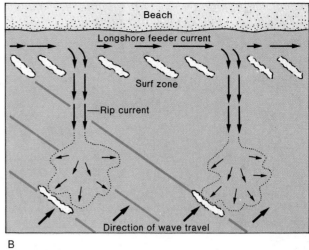

A

B

Formation of Rip Currents
Figure 14.7

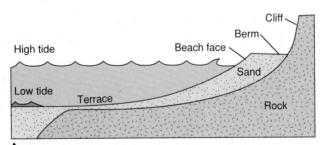

A
Parts of a Beach
Figure 14.9a

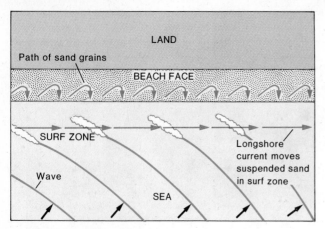

Longshore Drift of Sand
Figure 14.11

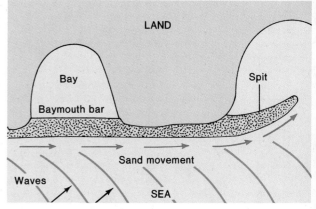

Formation of Baymouth Bars and Spits
Figure 14.12

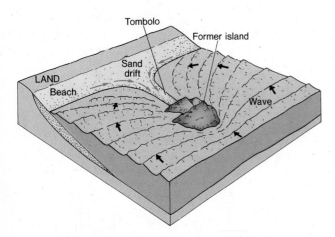

Formation of a Tombolo
Figure 14.15a

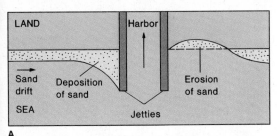

A

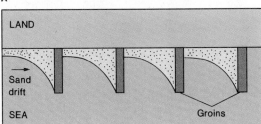

B

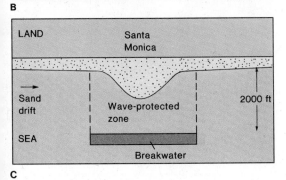

C

Effect of Jetties and Groins
Figure 14.16

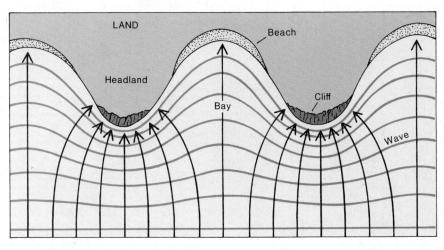

Wave Refraction of Irregular Coast
Figure 14.18a

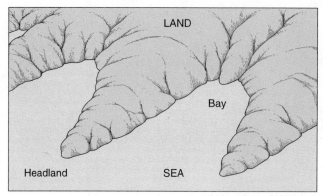

A

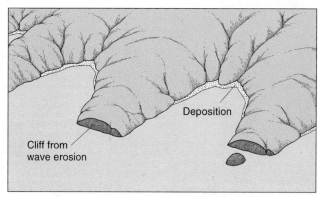

B

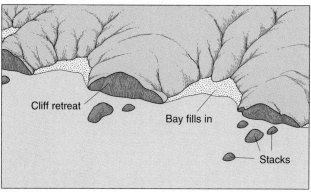

C

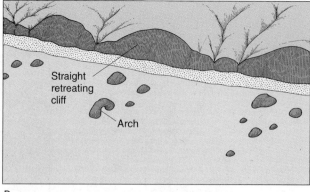

D

Straightening of Irregular Coast by Wave Erosion
Figure 14.19

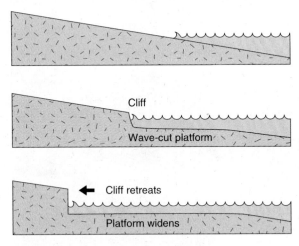

Development of a Wave-Cut Platform
Figure 14.21b

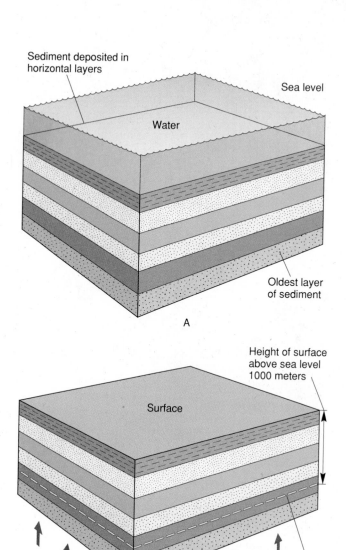

Sediment deposited in horizontal layers

Sea level

Water

Oldest layer of sediment

A

Height of surface above sea level 1000 meters

Surface

Sea level

Arrows represent uplift

B

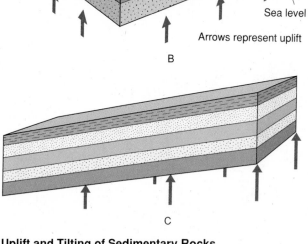

C

Uplift and Tilting of Sedimentary Rocks
Figure 15.6

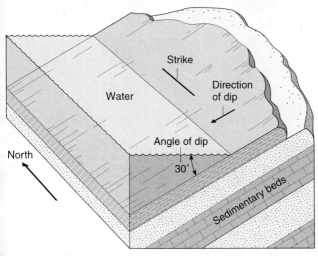

Strike and Dip
Figure 15.8

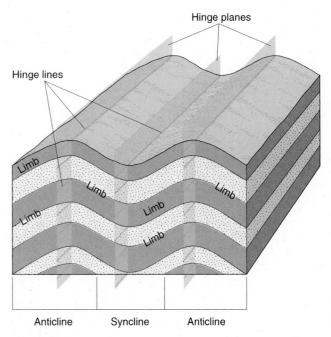

Anticlines and Synclines
Figure 15.13

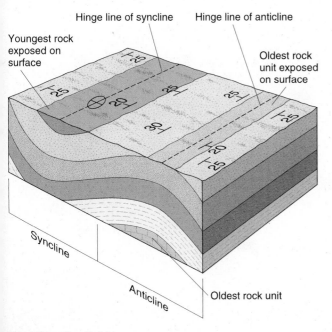

Non-Plunging Folds
Figure 15.14

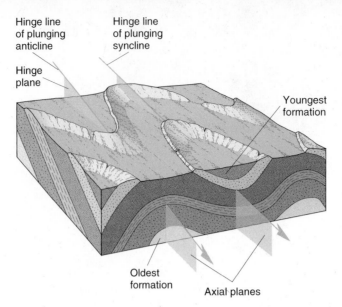

Hinge line
of plunging
anticline

Hinge line
of plunging
syncline

Hinge
plane

Youngest
formation

Oldest
formation

Axial planes

Plunging Folds
Figure 15.15

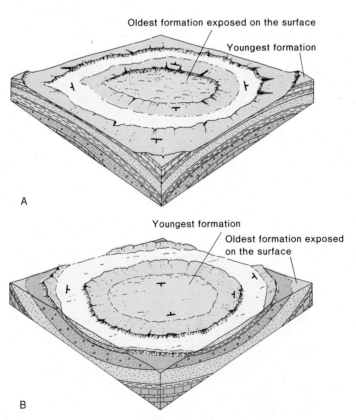

Oldest formation exposed on the surface

Youngest formation

A

Youngest formation

Oldest formation exposed
on the surface

B

Structural Dome and Structural Basin
Figure 15.17

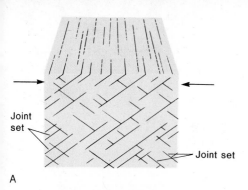

A

Joint
set

Joint set

A

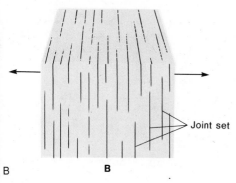

Joint set

B

B

Joint Sets
Figure 15.22

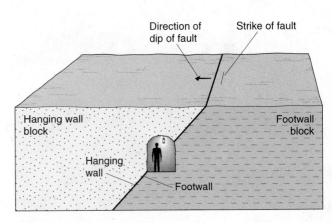

Direction of
dip of fault

Strike of fault

Hanging wall
block

Footwall
block

Hanging
wall

Footwall

Hanging Wall and Foot Wall
Figure 15.24

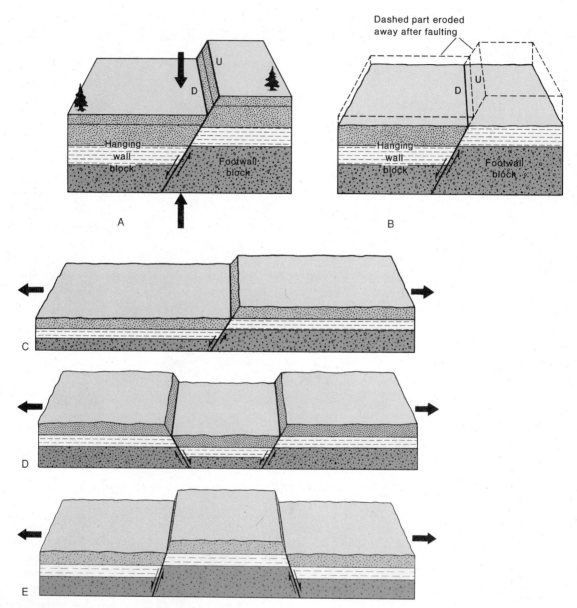

Normal Faults, Horsts and Grabens
Figure 15.25

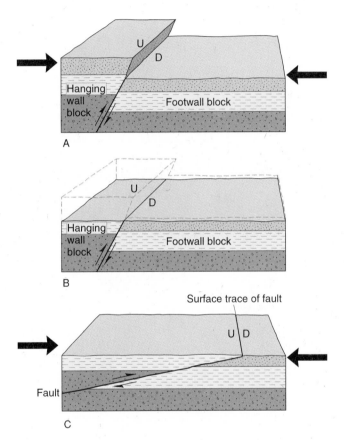

Reverse and Thrust Faults
Figure 15.27

A

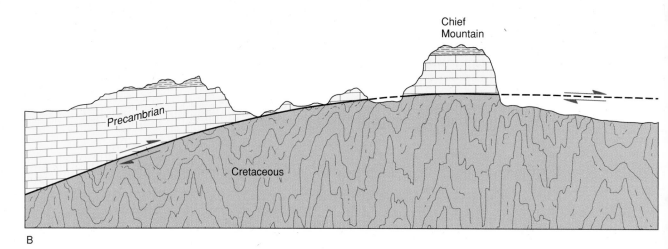

Chief
Mountain

Precambrian

Cretaceous

B

Chief Mountain
Figure 15.29

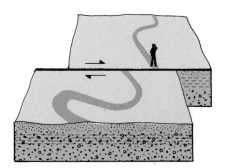

Right Lateral, Strike-Slip Fault
Figure 15.30

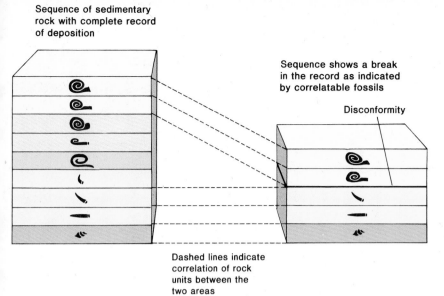

Sequence of sedimentary
rock with complete record
of deposition

Sequence shows a break
in the record as indicated
by correlatable fossils

Disconformity

Dashed lines indicate
correlation of rock
units between the
two areas

Representation of a Disconformity
Figure 15.31

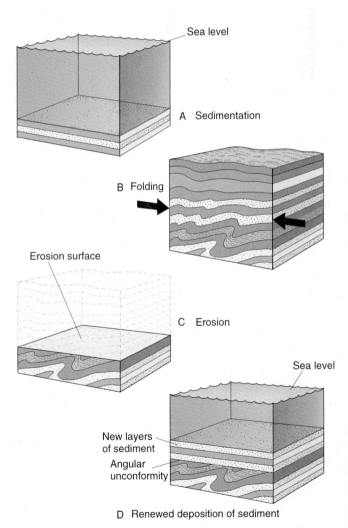

Sea level

A Sedimentation

B Folding

Erosion surface

C Erosion

New layers
of sediment

Angular
unconformity

Sea level

D Renewed deposition of sediment

Development of an Angular Unconformity
Figure 15.32

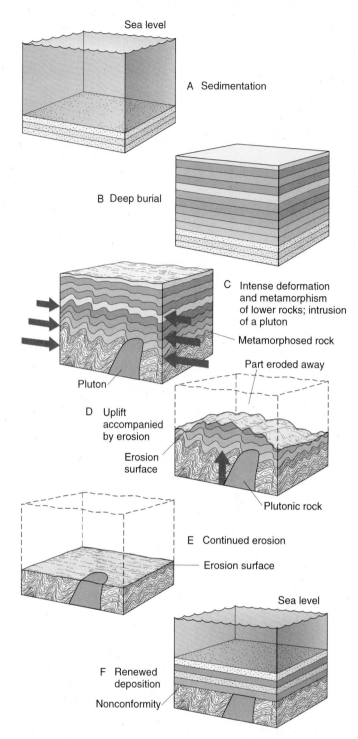

Sea level

A Sedimentation

B Deep burial

C Intense deformation
and metamorphism
of lower rocks; intrusion
of a pluton

Metamorphosed rock

Pluton

Part eroded away

D Uplift
accompanied
by erosion

Erosion
surface

Plutonic rock

E Continued erosion

Erosion surface

Sea level

F Renewed
deposition

Nonconformity

Development of a Nonconformity
Figure 15.35

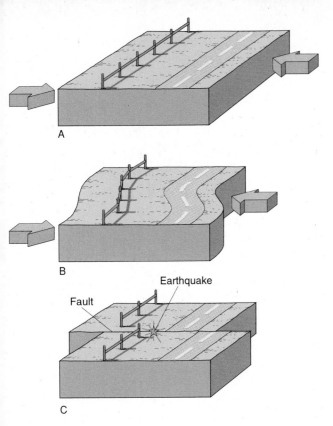

A

B

Earthquake

Fault

C

Elastic Rebound Theory
Figure 16.2

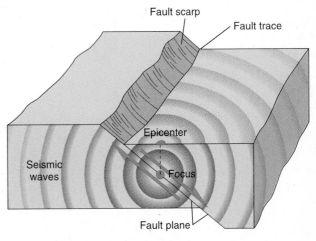

Fault scarp

Fault trace

Epicenter

Seismic
waves

Focus

Fault plane

Earthquake Focus and Epicenter
Figure 16.4

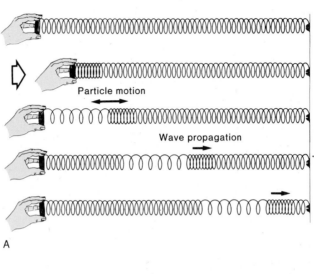

Particle motion

Wave propagation

A

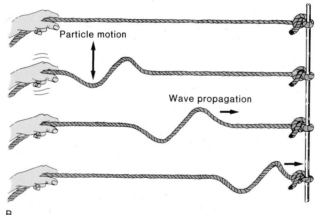

Particle motion

Wave propagation

B

Particle Motion in Seismic Waves
Figure 16.5

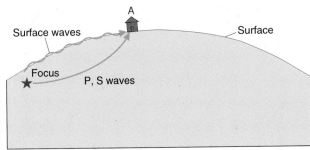

A Station near focus

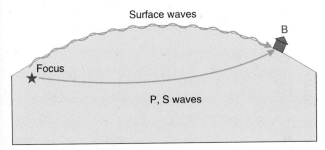

B Station far from focus

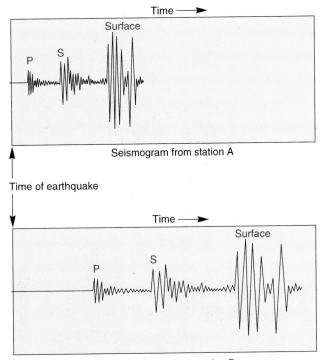

Time of earthquake

Seismogram from station A

Seismogram from station B

P-Wave, S-Wave and Surface Wave Intervals
Figure 16.8

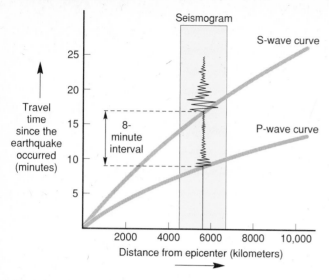

Time-Travel Curve
Figure 16.9

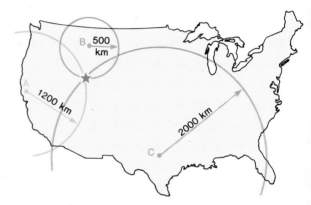

Locating an Earthquake Epicenter
Figure 16.10

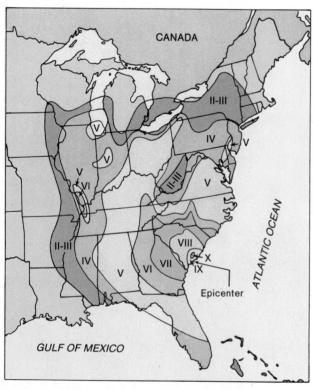

Intensity Map—1886 Charleston Earthquake
Figure 16.11

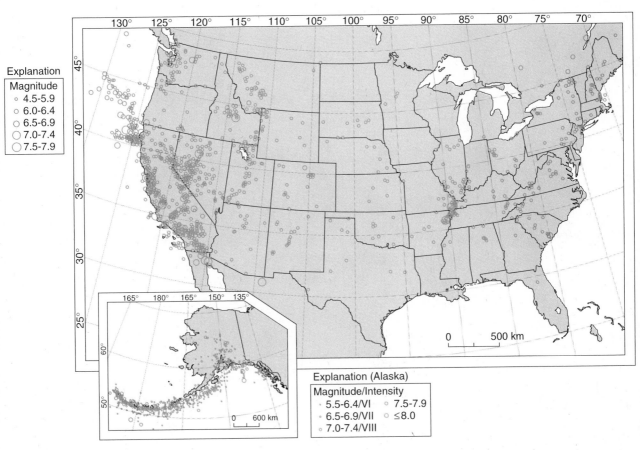

Earthquake Epicenters (M /gtn/ 4.5) in the U.S.
Figure 16.12

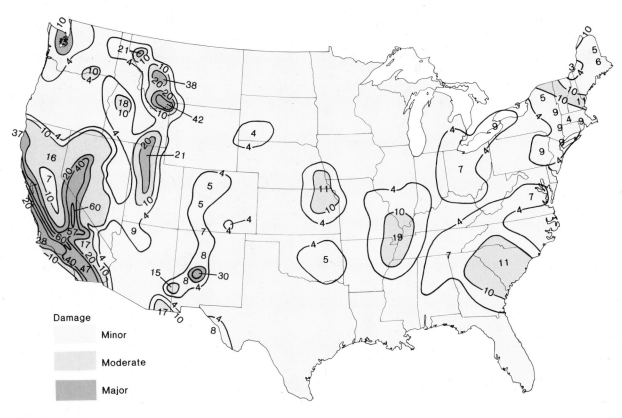

1976 Map of Seismic Risk
Figure 16.13

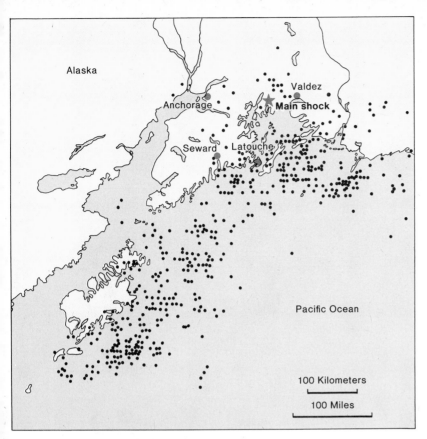

Aftershocks—1964 Alaska Earthquake
Figure 16.18

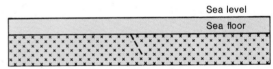

A Before earthquake

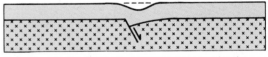

B Sudden displacement of sea floor causes sea level to drop momentarily

C Water rushes into depression and overcorrects, raising sea level slightly

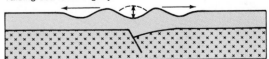

D Sea level oscillates before coming to rest; long, low waves (tsunamis) are sent out over sea surface

Generation of a Tsunamis
Figure 16.20

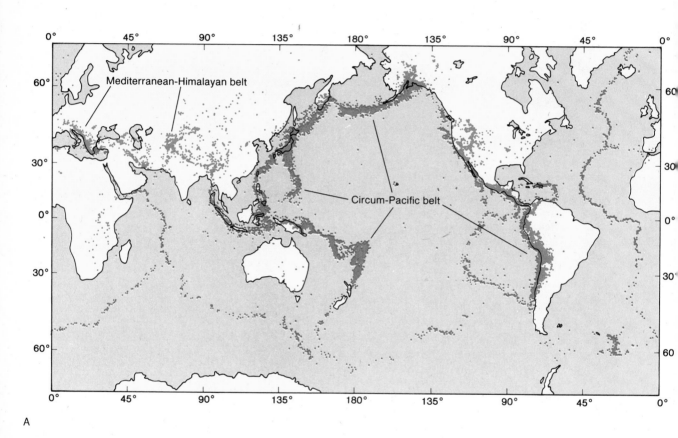

A

World Distribution of Earthquakes (0-700 km)
Figure 16.22a

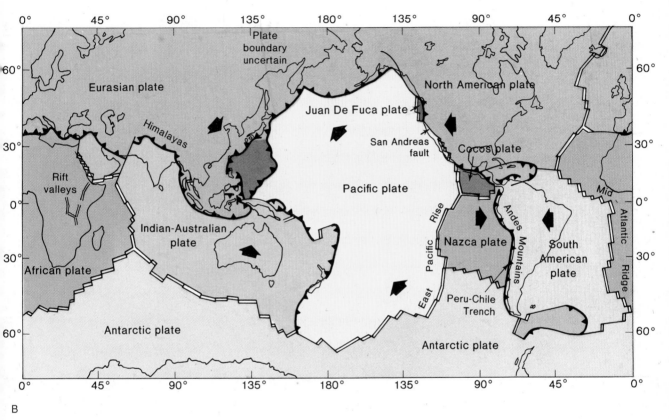

B

Major Plates of the World
Figure 16.22b

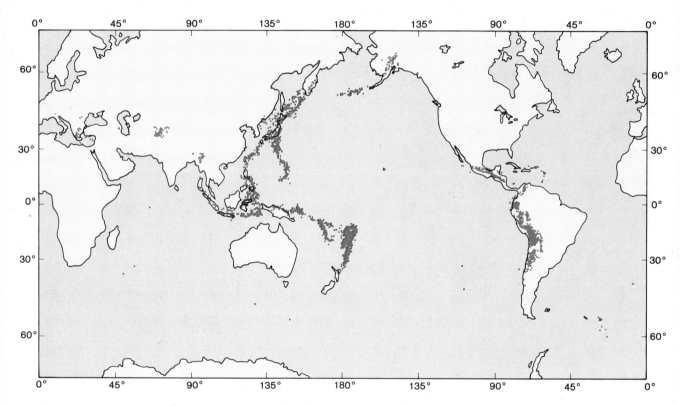

World Distribution of Earthquakes (100-700 km)
Figure 16.23

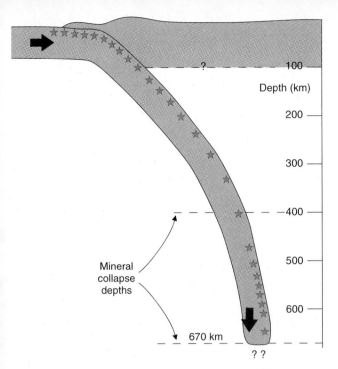

Earthquake Distribution at Convergent Boundary
Figure 16.33

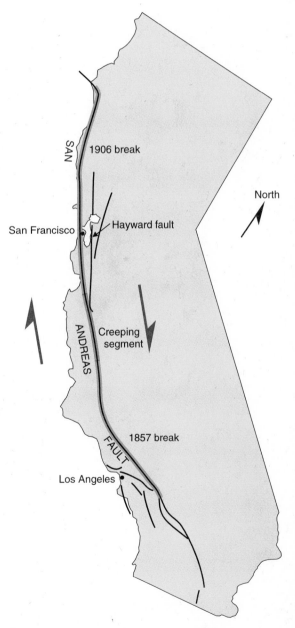

Seismic Gaps Along San Andreas Fault
Figure Box 16.2;1

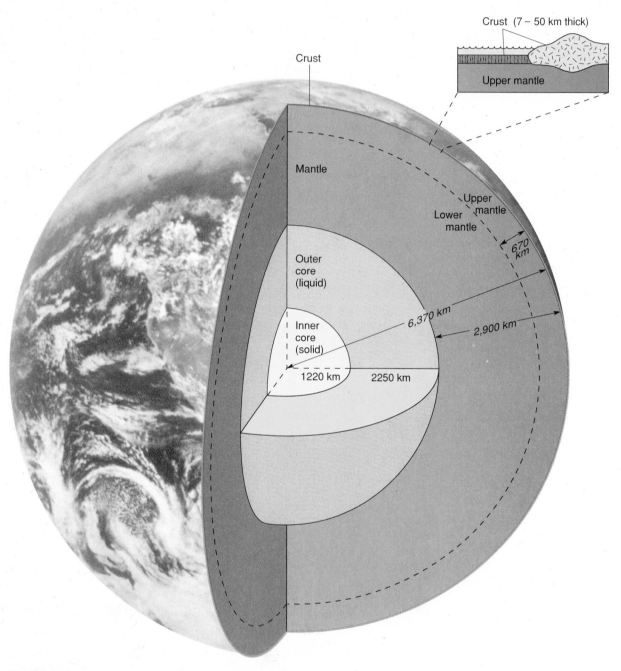

Crust (7 – 50 km thick)

Upper mantle

Crust

Mantle

Outer core (liquid)

Inner core (solid)

Upper mantle

Lower mantle

670 km

6,370 km

2,900 km

1220 km

2250 km

Earth Interior
Figure 17.5

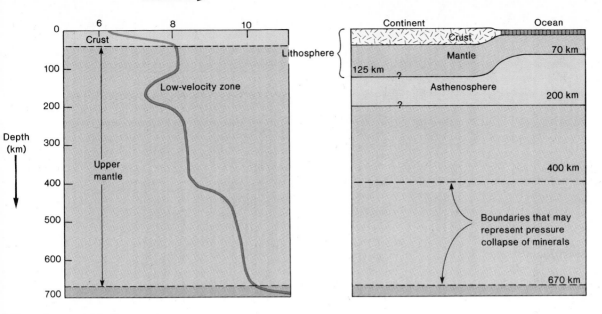

Lithosphere and Asthenosphere
Figure 17.7

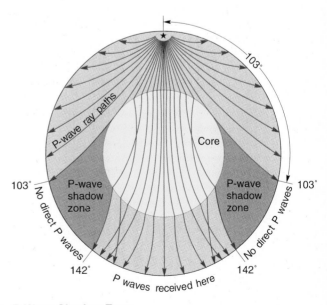

P-Wave Shadow Zone
Figure 17.8

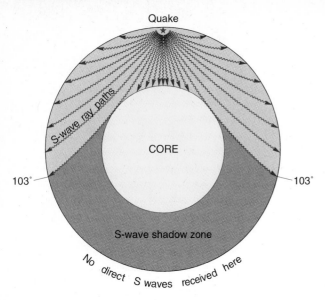

S-Wave Shadow Zone
Figure 17.9

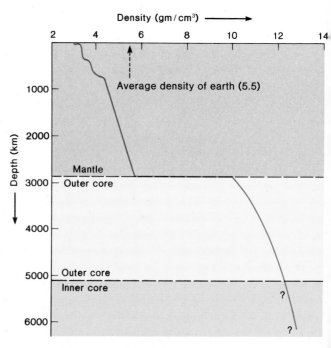

Density Variations with Depth
Figure 17.10

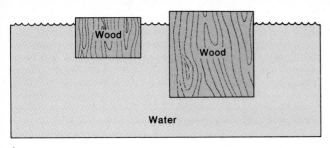

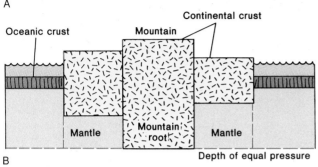

A

B

Isostatic Balance
Figure 17.11

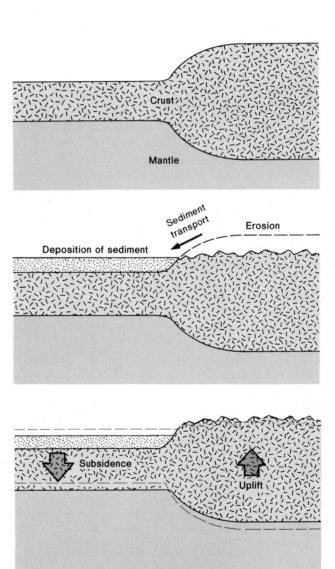

Isostatic Adjustment of Crust
Figure 17.12

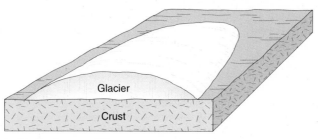

A **Glacier forms, adding weight to crust**

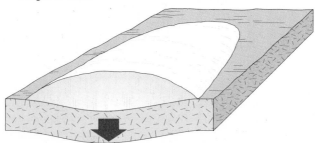

B **Subsidence due to weight of ice**

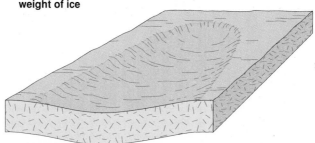

C **Ice melts, removing weight from crust**

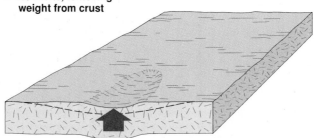

D **Crustal rebound as crust rises toward original position**

Crustal Rebound Following Glacier Retreat
Figure 17.13

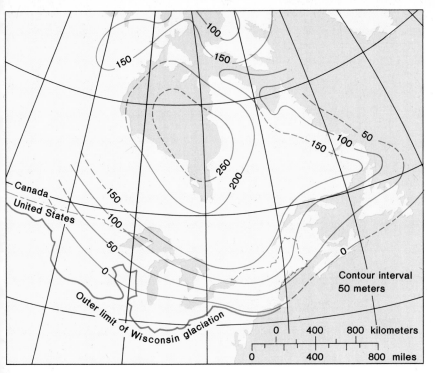

Crustal Rebound in North America
Figure 17.14

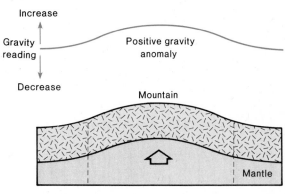

Positive Gravity Anomaly
Figure 17.19

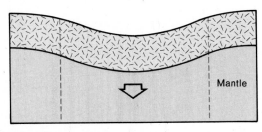

Negative Gravity Anomaly
Figure 17.20

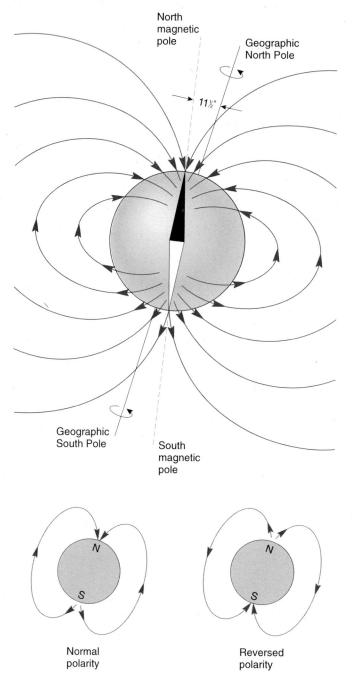

Earth's Magnetic Field
Figure 17.21

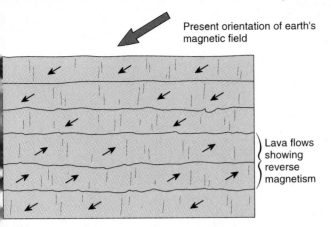

Present orientation of earth's magnetic field

Lava flows showing reverse magnetism

Stacked Lava Flows and Magnetic Reversals
Figure 17.23

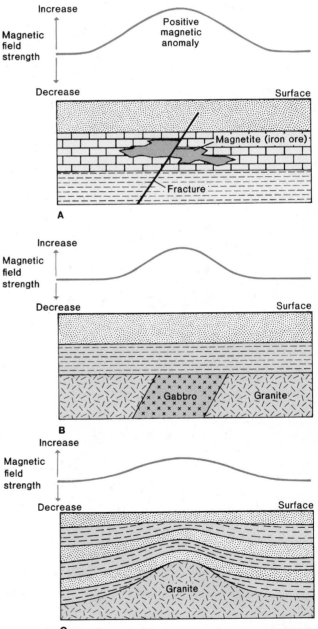

Increase

Magnetic field strength

Decrease

Positive magnetic anomaly

Surface

Magnetite (iron ore)

Fracture

A

Increase

Magnetic field strength

Decrease

Surface

Gabbro   Granite

B

Increase

Magnetic field strength

Decrease

Surface

Granite

C
Positive Magnetic Anomalies
Figure 17.25

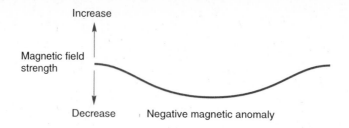

Increase

Magnetic field
strength

Decrease   Negative magnetic anomaly

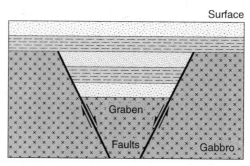

Surface

Graben

Faults   Gabbro

Negative Magnetic Anomaly
Figure 17.26

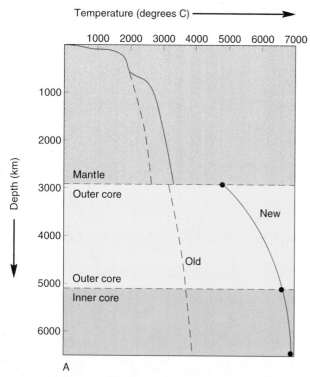

Temperature (degrees C)

1000 2000 3000 4000 5000 6000 7000

Depth (km)

1000

2000

3000 Mantle
      Outer core

4000   New

5000 Old
      Outer core
5000 Inner core

6000

A

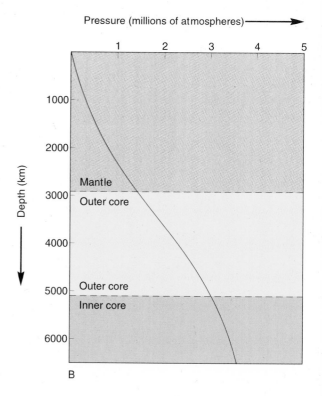

Pressure (millions of atmospheres)

1   2   3   4   5

Depth (km)

1000

2000

3000 Mantle
      Outer core

4000

5000 Outer core
      Inner core

6000

B

Temperature and Pressure Distribution with Depth
Figure 17.27

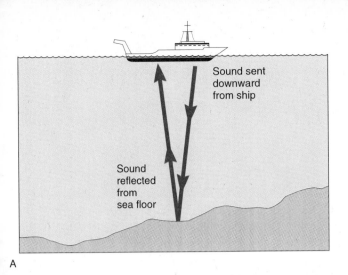

A

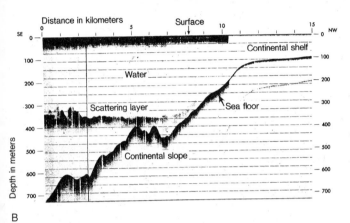

B

Echo Sounding of Continental Margin
Figure 18.3

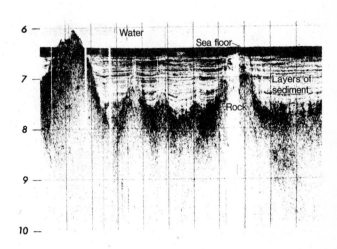

Seismic Profile of Abyssal Plain
Figure 18.4

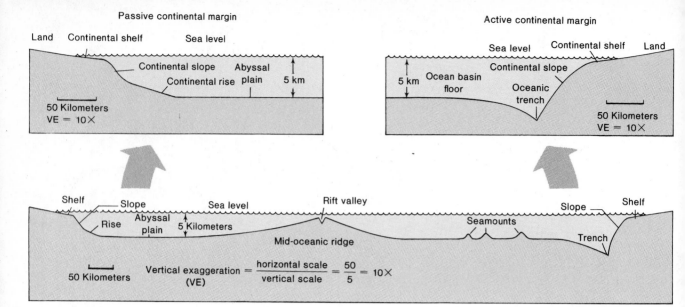

Profiles of Sea Floor Topography
Figure 18.6

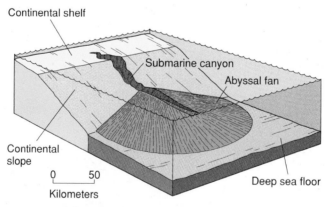

Submarine Canyon and Abyssal Fan
Figure 18.9

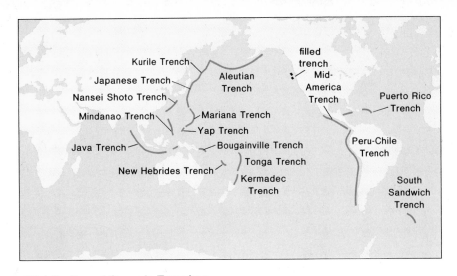

Distribution of Oceanic Trenches
Figure 18.13

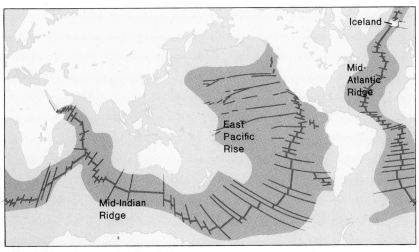

Mid-Ocean Ridges and Fracture Zones
Figure 18.15

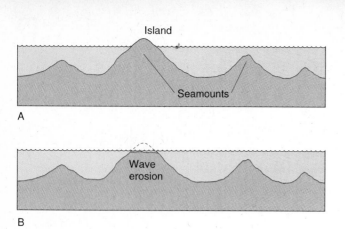

A

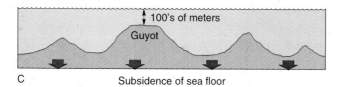

B

C

Seamounts and Guyots
Figure 18.20

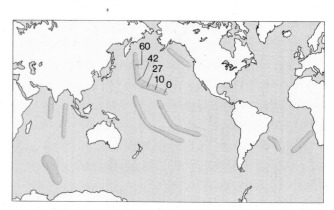

Distribution of Aseismic Ridges
Figure 18.21

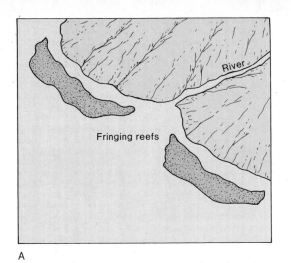

A

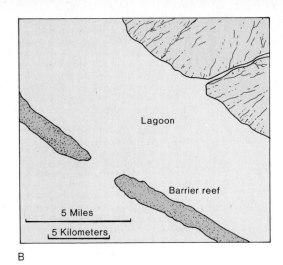

B

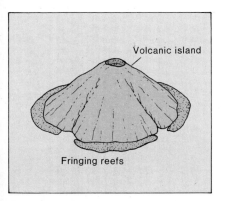

C

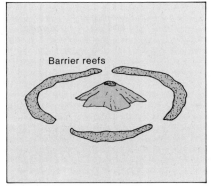

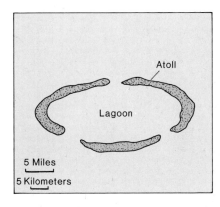

Types of Reefs
Figure 18.22

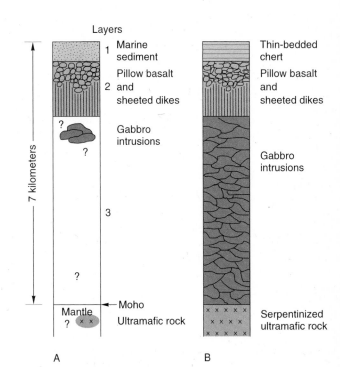

A

B

Oceanic Crust and Ophiolite Sequence
Figure 18.25

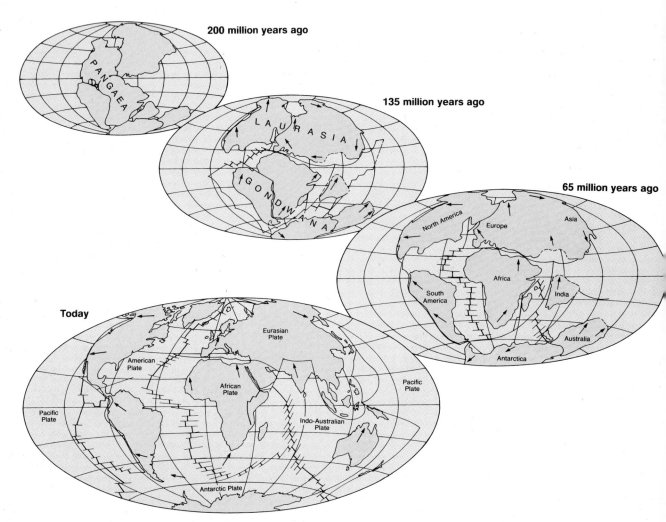

200 million years ago

135 million years ago

65 million years ago

Today

Break-Up of Pangaea and Continental Drift
Figure 19.2

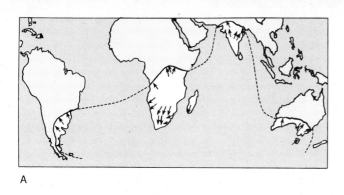

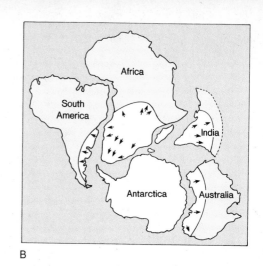

Distribution of Late Paleozoic Glaciations
Figure 19.3

A Rock near north
magnetic pole

B Rock near equator in
northern hemisphere

C Rock in southern
hemisphere

Magnetic Inclination and Latitude
Figure 19.8

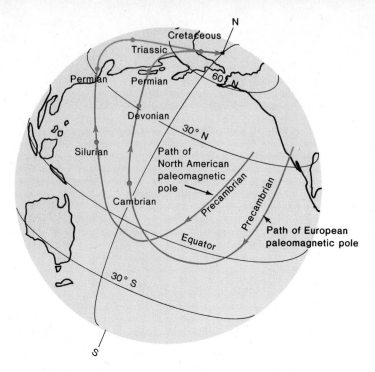

Polar Wandering Curves
Figure 19.10

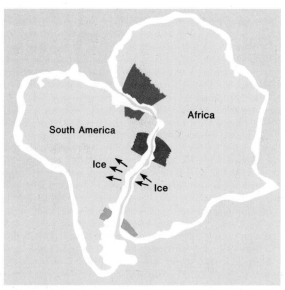

Matching Geology of Africa and South America
Figure 19.11

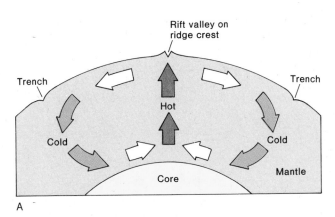

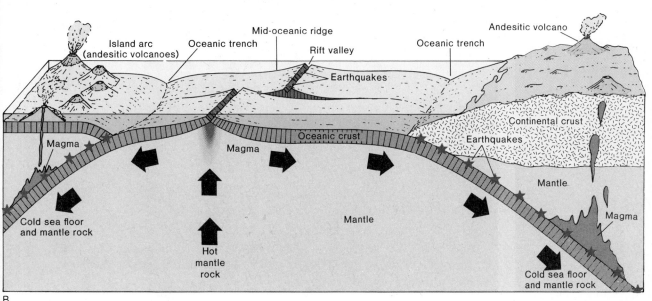

Sea-Floor Spreading
Figure 19.12

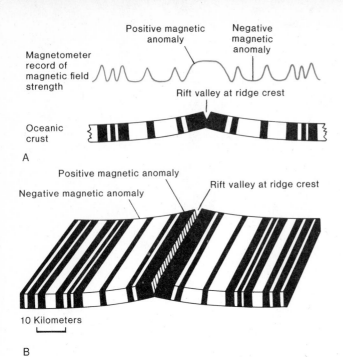

Positive magnetic anomaly

Negative magnetic anomaly

Magnetometer record of magnetic field strength

Positive magnetic anomaly

Negative magnetic anomaly

Rift valley at ridge crest

Oceanic crust

A

Positive magnetic anomaly

Rift valley at ridge crest

Negative magnetic anomaly

10 Kilometers

B

Marine Magnetic Anomalies
Figure 19.14

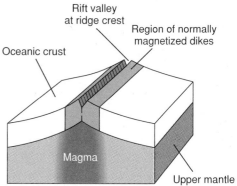

Rift valley at ridge crest

Region of normally magnetized dikes

Oceanic crust

Magma

Upper mantle

A Time of normal magnetism

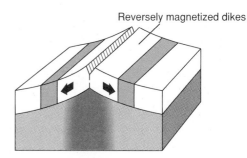

Reversely magnetized dikes

B Time of reverse magnetism

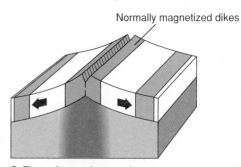

Normally magnetized dikes

C Time of normal magnetism

Origin of Marine Magnetic Anomalies
Figure 19.16

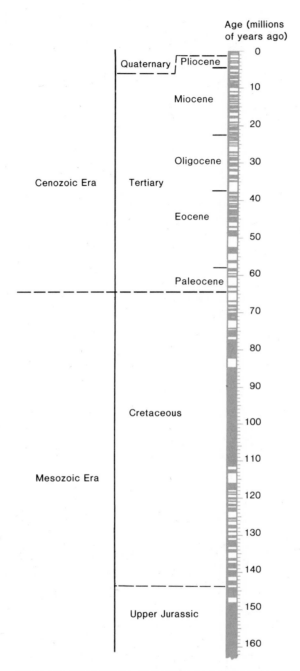

Magnetic Time Scale: Mesozoic and Cenozoic Eras
Figure 19.18

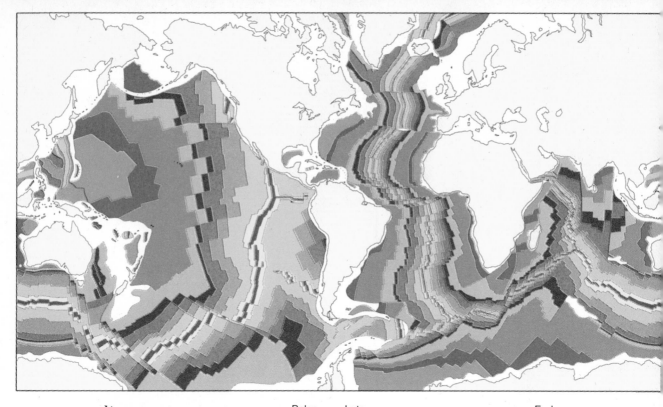

Age Map of the Sea Floor
Figure 19.19

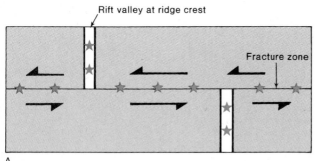

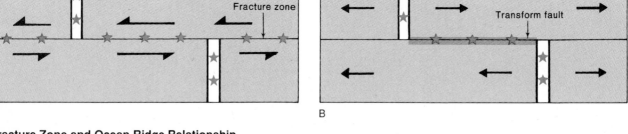

Fracture Zone and Ocean Ridge Relationship
Figure 19.20

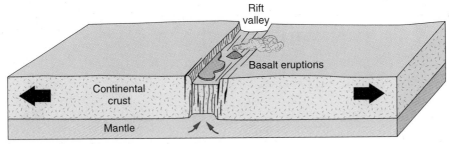

A Continent undergoes extension. The crust is thinned and
a rift valley forms (East African Rift Valleys).

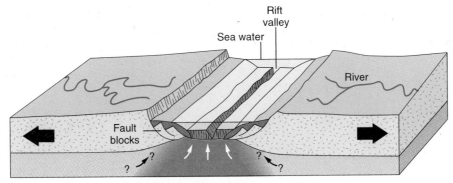

B Continent tears in two. Continent edges are faulted and uplifted.
Basalt eruptions form oceanic crust (Red Sea).

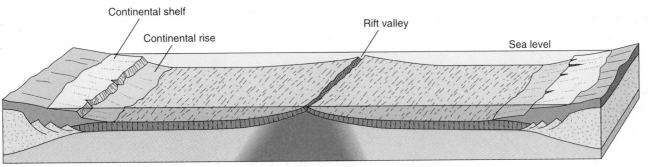

C Continental sediments blanket the subsiding margins to form continental shelves and rises.
The ocean widens and a mid–oceanic ridge develops (Atlantic Ocean).

Continent Rifting and a Spreading Ocean
Figure 19.22

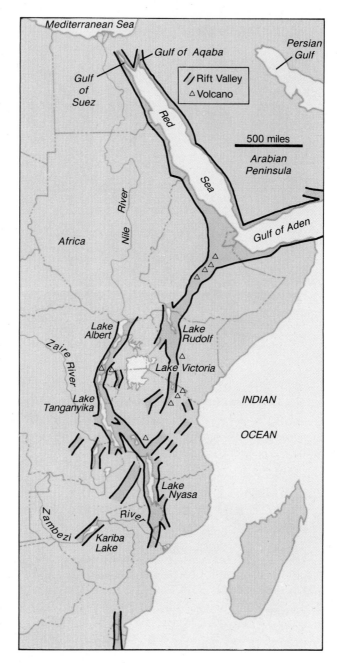

East African Rift Valleys and the Red Sea
Figure 19.23

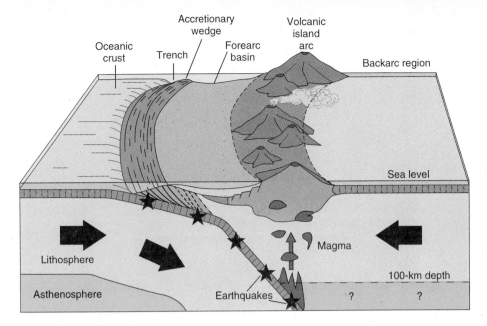

Ocean-Ocean Convergence
Figure 19.29

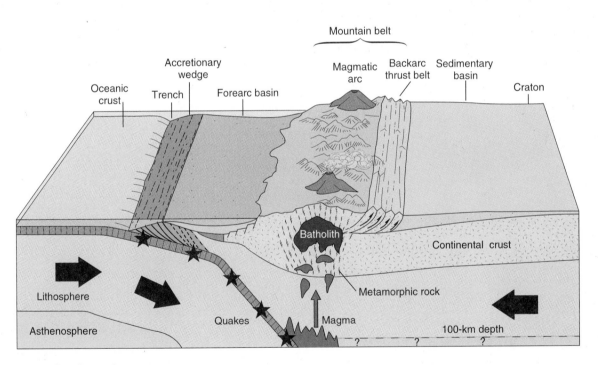

Ocean-Continent Convergence
Figure 19.33

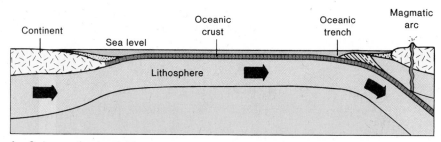

A Ocean-continent convergence

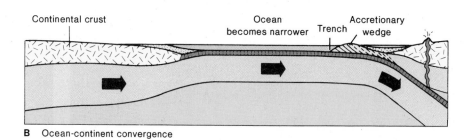

B Ocean-continent convergence

C Continent-continent collision

Continent-Continent Collision
Figure 19.34

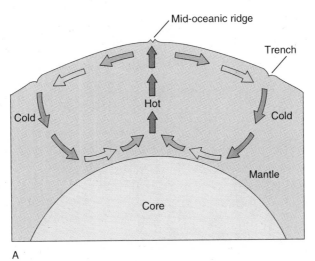

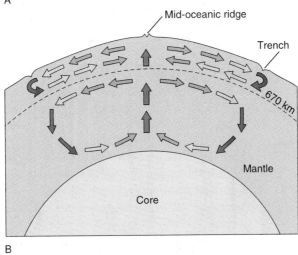

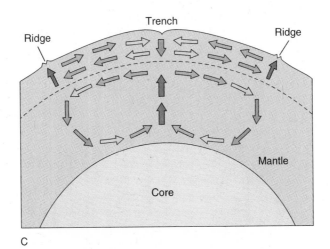

Models of Mantle Convection
Figure 19.38

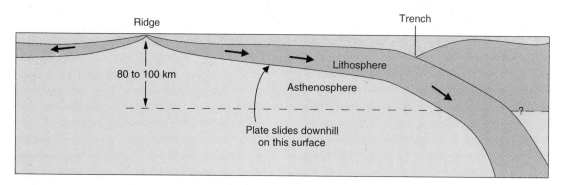

Ridge Push
Figure 19.39

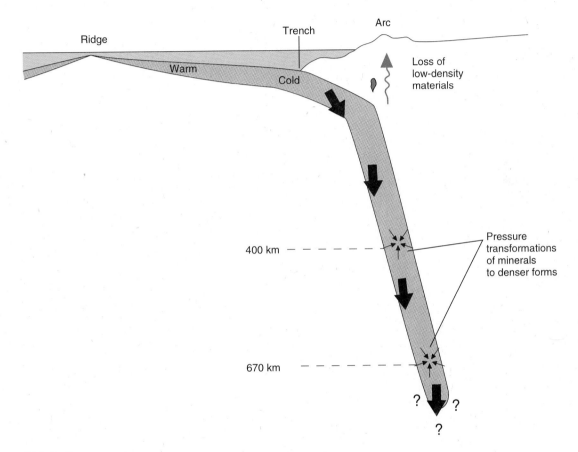

Slab Pull
Figure 19.40

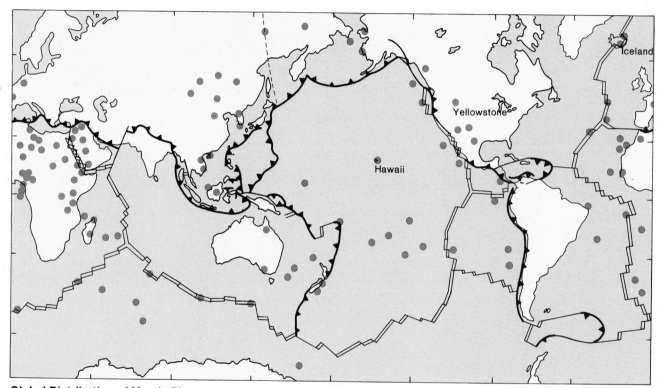

Global Distribution of Mantle Plumes
Figure 19.43

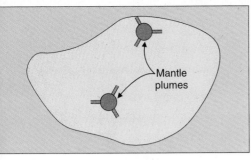

A

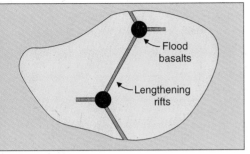

B

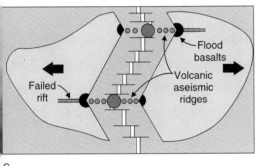

C

Continental Break-Up by Mantle Plumes
Figure 19.46

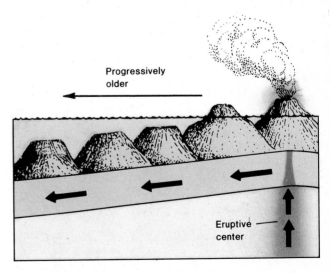

Sea Floor Moving Over a Mantle Plume
Figure 19.47

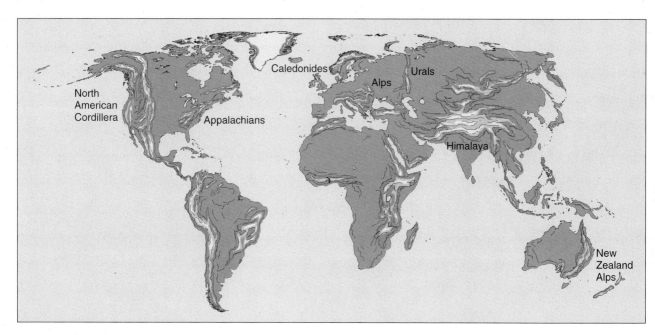

Major Mountain Belts of the World
Figure 20.2

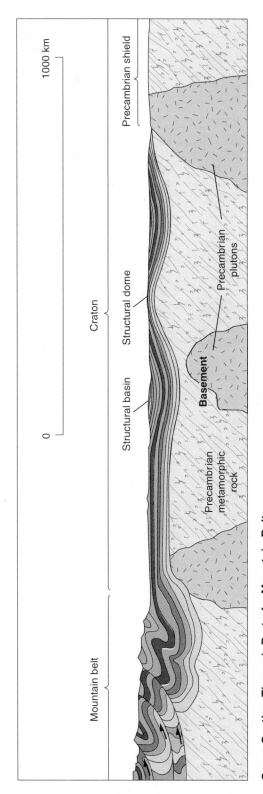

Cross Section Through Part of a Mountain Belt
Figure 20.4

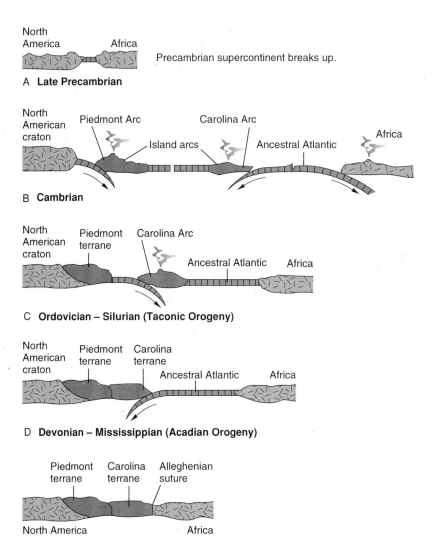

North
America   Africa

Precambrian supercontinent breaks up.

A **Late Precambrian**

North
American craton   Piedmont Arc   Carolina Arc   Africa

Island arcs   Ancestral Atlantic

B **Cambrian**

North
American craton   Piedmont terrane   Carolina Arc   Ancestral Atlantic   Africa

C **Ordovician – Silurian (Taconic Orogeny)**

North
American craton   Piedmont terrane   Carolina terrane   Ancestral Atlantic   Africa

D **Devonian – Mississippian (Acadian Orogeny)**

Piedmont terrane   Carolina terrane   Alleghenian suture

North America   Africa

E **Pennsylvanian – Permian (Alleghenian Orogeny)
North America and Africa joined**

North America   Alleghenian suture   Africa

F **Triassic – Rifting begins. Breakup of Pangea starts**

Formation of the Appalachian Mountain Belt
Figure 20.14

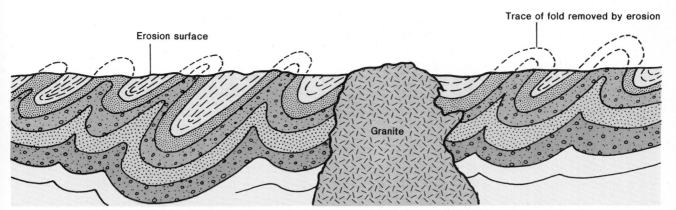

A Before block faulting. Folding and intrusion of a pluton during an orogeny has been followed by a period of erosion.

Erosion surface

Trace of fold removed by erosion

Granite

0   10 Kilometers

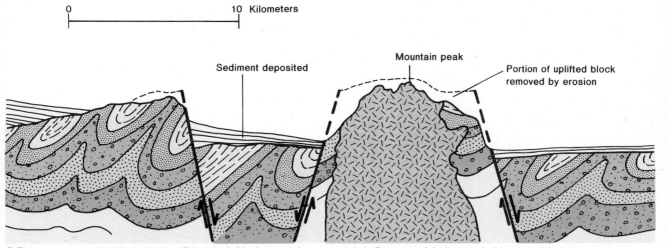

Sediment deposited

Mountain peak

Portion of uplifted block removed by erosion

B The same area after block-faulting. Tilted fault-block mountain range on left. Range to right is bounded by normal faults.

Development of Fault-Block Mountains
Figure 20.16

Central part of mountain belt

Continental crust

Lithosphere mantle

Asthenosphere

A Thick continental crust of a mountain belt produced
during orogeny.

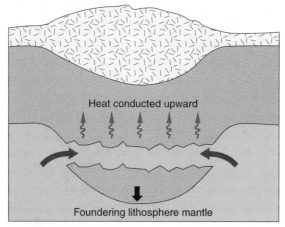

Heat conducted upward

Foundering lithosphere mantle

B Delamination of gravitationally unstable lithosphere
mantle. Hot asthenosphere flows into place and heats
overlying lithosphere.

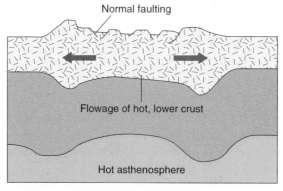

Normal faulting

Flowage of hot, lower crust

Hot asthenosphere

C Extension with hot lower crust flowing outward.

Delamination and Thinning of Continental Crust
Figure 20.20

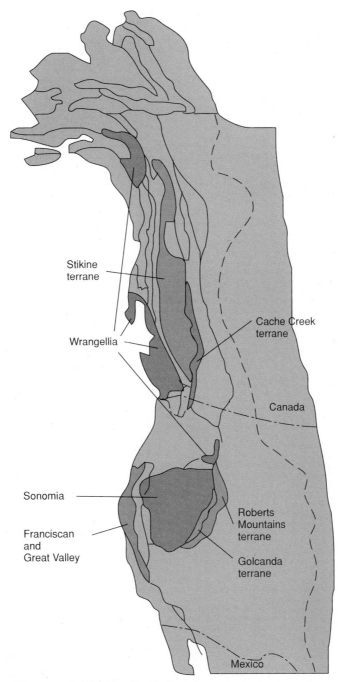

Terranes in Western North America
Figure 20.21

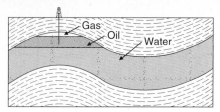

A Anticline

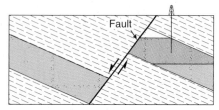

B Normal fault

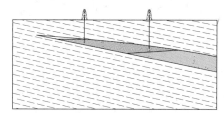

C Thrust fault

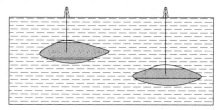

D Sandstone lenses

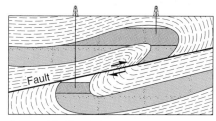

E Sandstone pinchout

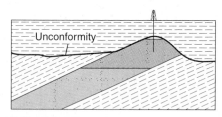

F Unconformity

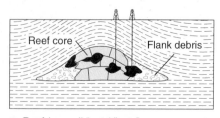

G Reef (a small "patch" reef)

Traps for Oil and Gas
Figure 21.2

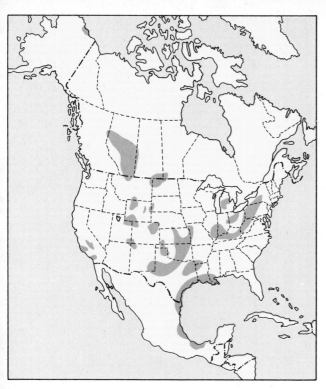

Major Oil Fields of North America
Figure 21.3

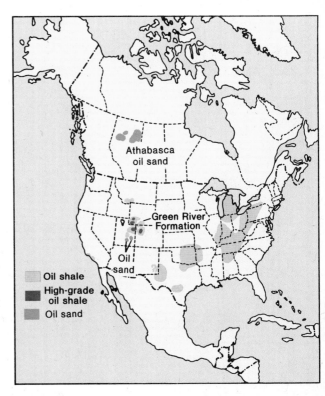

Athabasca
oil sand

Green River
Formation

Oil
sand

Oil shale

High-grade
oil shale

Oil sand

Major Oil Sands and Shales of North America
Figure 21.6

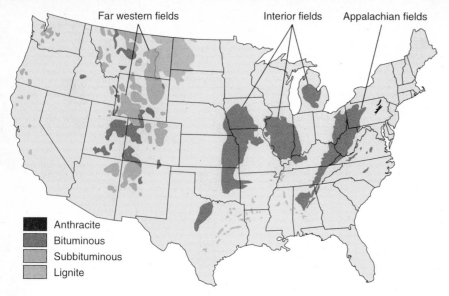

Coal Fields of the United States
Figure 21.11

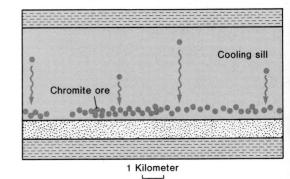

Formation of Chromite Deposit
Figure 21.12

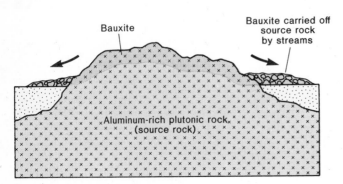

Formation of a Bauxite Deposit
Figure 21.18

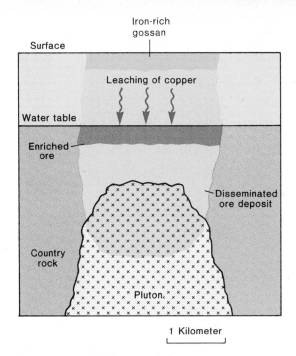

Supergene Enrichment of Copper
Figure 21.19

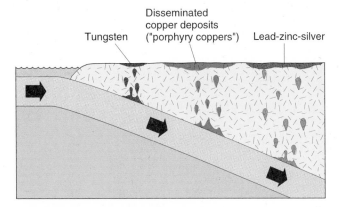

Metallic Ores and Plate Subduction
Figure 21.24

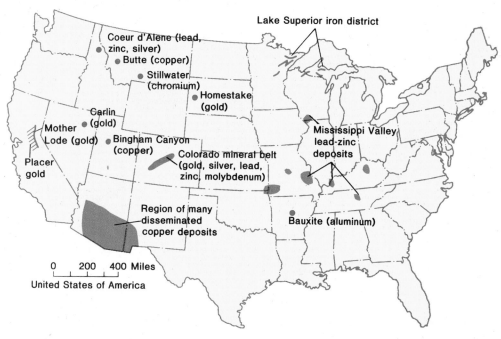

Metallic Ore Deposits of the U.S.
Figure 21.27

Credits

Line Art

Figure 1.10 Source: W. Hamilton, U.S. Geological Survey

Figure 2.20 From R. D. Dallmeyer, *Physical Geology Laboratory Manual.* Copyright © 1978 Kendall Hunt Publishing Company, Dubuque, IA. Reprinted with permission.

Figure 3.4 Source: C. Bacon, U.S. Geological Survey.

Figure 5.22 Source: U.S. Department of Agriculture.

Figure 7.16 From W. G. Ernst, *Metamorphism and Plate Tectonic Regimes.* Copyright © 1975 Dowden, Hutchinson & Ross, Stroudsberg, PA. Reprinted with permission.

Box 7.3;1 From W. G. Ernst, *Metamorphism and Plate Tectonic Regimes.* Copyright © 1975 Dowden, Hutchinson & Ross, Stroudsberg, PA. Reprinted with permission.

Box 7.3;2 From W. G. Ernst, *Metamorphism and Plate Tectonic Regimes.* Copyright © 1975 Dowden, Hutchinson & Ross, Stroudsberg, PA. Reprinted with permission.

Figure 8.21 Source: Geological Society of America.

Figure 8.22 Source: U.S. Geological Survey Publication *Geologic Time.*

Figure 9.4 Source: C. F. S. Sharpe

Figure 11.27 Source: Modified from W. R. Keefer, *U.S. Geological Survey Bulletin,* p. 1347, 1971.

Figure 12.33 Source: After C. S. Denny, *U.S. Geolgical Survey National Atlas of the United States.*

Figure 12.34 Sources: C. S. Denny, U.S. Geolgical Survey, and the Geological Map of North America, Geological Society of America, and The Geological Survey of Canada.

Figure 13.3 Source: U.S. Department of Agriculture.

Figure 13.20 Source: U.S. Bureau of Reclamation, 1960.

Figure 16.13 Source: U.S. Geological Survey

Figure 16.18 Source: U.S. Geological Survey

Figure 16.22a From Barazangi and Dorman, *Bulletin of Seismological Society of America,* 1969.

Figure 16.22b Source: W. Hamilton, U.S. Geological Survey.

Figure 16.23 From Barazangi and Dorman, *Bulletin of Seismological Society of America,* 1969.

Box 16.2;1 Source: U.S. Geological Survey

Figure 17.14 From Phillip B. King, "Tectonics of Quaternary Time in Middle North America," in *The Quaternary of the United States,* H. C. Wright, Jr. and David G. Frey, eds., fig. 4A, p. 836. Reprinted by permission of Princeton University Press.

Figure 18.21 Source: W. Jason Morgan, *Geological Society of America Memoir, 132,* and other sources. 1972.

Figure 19.2 From American Petroleum Institute.

Figure 19.3 Source: Arthur Holmes, *Principles of Physical Geology,* 2d. ed., 1965. Ronald Press, New York, NY.

Figure 19.10 From A. Cox and R. R. Doell, *Geological Society of America Bulletin,* 1960.

Figure 19.18 Source: Modified from R. L. Larson and W. C. Pitman, III, *Geological Society of America Bulletin,* 1972.

Figure 19.29 From W. R. Dickinson, *Island Arcs, Deep Sea Trenches, and Back-Arc Basins,* pp. 33–40. Copyright © 1977 American Geophysical Union.

Figure 19.34a From W. R. Dickinson, *Island Arcs, Deep Sea Trenches, and Back-Arc Basins,* pp. 33–40. Copyright © 1977 American Geophysical Union.

Figure 19.43 Source: W. S. F. Kidd and K. Burke, SUNY at Albany.

Figure 20.20 Sources: J. F. Dewey, "Extensional Collapse of Orogens," in *Tectonics,* 7:1123–1139, 1988; and K. D. Nelson, "Are Crustal Thickness Variations in Old Mountain Belts Like the Appalachians a Consequence of Lithospheric Delamination?" in *Geology,* 20:498–502, 1992.

Figure 20.21 Source: U.S. Geological Survey Open File Map 83–716.

Figure 21.6 Source: U.S. Geological Survey

Figure 21.11 Source: U.S. Geological Survey

Photo Credit

Figure 1.5 © Erwin Raisz; Courtesy of Raisz Landform maps, P.O. Box 2254, Jamaica Plain, MA. 02130

Figure 1.5 © Erwin Raisz; Courtesy of Raisz Landform maps, P.O. Box 2254, Jamaica Plain, MA 02130

Figure 1.8 Photo by NASA

Figure 2.1A Photo by C. C. Plummer

Figure 11.1B Photo by David McGeary

Figure 12.12 Photo by U.S. Geological Survey

Figure 15.29A Photo by Frank H. Hanna

Figure 17.5B Photo by NASA